MASTERY OF THE MIND

Conquer Procrastination, Crush Anxiety, And Obliterate 17 Other Mental Wastes To Take Control Of Your Mind, And Take Control Of Your Life

Noam Lightstone

Legal Notice

Disclaimer

All attempts have been made to verify the information in this book; however, neither the author nor the publisher assumes any responsibility for errors, omissions, or contrary interpretations of the content within.

Neither the publisher nor the individual author shall be liable for any physical, psychological, emotional, financial, or commercial damages, including, but not limited to, special, incidental, consequential or other damages on behalf of the purchaser or reader of this book.

The information provided in this book is designed to provide helpful information on the subjects discussed. This book is not meant to be used, nor should it be used, to diagnose or treat any medical condition. For diagnosis or treatment of any medical problem, consult your own physician. The publisher and author are not responsible for any specific health needs that may require medical supervision and are not liable for any damages or negative consequences from any treatment, action, application or preparation, to any person reading or following the information in this book.

VI

Table of Contents

Conclusion

Extras

Dedication

To the journey of learning—may I never stop.

And to everyone who has supported and helped me over the years.

Thank you.

Acknowledgments

Thank you to all my friends and family for being there for me.

Special thanks to Ryan and Rico, who were very supportive during the writing of this book and who offered useful criticism and feedback... as well as good times away from the keyboard to let off some steam. Also thanks to Patty for being my personal cheerleader at the end of the book writing.

I also thank my external team who helped me with editing, cover design, and formatting – Matt, Angie, Lawton, and Marley.

Professional photograph of Noam Lightstone in the biography section courtesy of Kat Ziger, and kzigerphotos.com.

Your Free Bonus

I don't know about you, but I'm not a fan of negative feelings. But they are a part of life. You can't get rid of them, but you can learn ways to deal with them so you feel better again.

As a way of saying thanks for buying my book, I'm offering a **free** tool that is exclusive to the readers of *Mastery Of The Mind*:

A lot of people are not *aware* of the habits, thought processes, or tools that are available to deal with negative behaviors. These negative behaviors include over thinking, spiraling, anxiety, and other really nasty things that suck your mental energy dry and lead to negative feelings. You have to figure out what works for you, but having some idea of the things you can try is very helpful. **Knowledge is power**. And if the knowledge helps you feel happy again, I say go for it.

I have written a PDF called *"The 20-Step Management Plan To Get Back To Crushing Life When You Are In Your Head, Anxious, Overwhelmed, Or Feeling Down"* that provides you with a step-by-step process of what you can do and how you can talk to yourself to stop feeling bad, get help, and confidently move forward in life. This is a plan I **created for myself** to help me in my personal life, but I am **sharing it with you**! It's helped me a lot and I know it will help you too.

You can download your **FREE** bonus here:

http://www.lightwayofthinking.com/mastery-of-the-mind-free-bonus

Mastery Of The Mind

xx

Section I

Beginning

Chapter 1.
Introduction

"*I want to do more and be happier in life*" is something we all think and say. So why do we continue to sabotage ourselves?

"I want to have more focus."

"I want to have more energy."

"I want to be more calm and relaxed."

You might be sabotaging yourself right now, in this very moment. You probably don't even realize it. You aren't aware of how you're shooting yourself in the foot, wasting valuable mental resources that can't be reclaimed once they've been spent. You already have enough stress, yet you continue to do these things.

Do you know how much lighter you could be? How much clearer you could think, how much more you could accomplish, how much happier you could be if you were just aware?

Thermodynamics is a branch of physics related to the study of energy, and associated with it are several principles. One of these laws, The First Law Of Thermodynamics, states that:

"Energy cannot be created or destroyed, it can only change form."

My philosophy is that we all have the same level of mental energy. However, because of certain beliefs, habits, and the environment you place yourself in or grew up in, you might have more or less available than someone else.

3

The goals of this book are to help you:

1. Identify the possible ways you might be wasting your mental energy, giving you the awareness that you need.

2. Learn a bit about where the mental wastes come from in your past and from your psychological makeup.

3. Find out what the positive alternatives are to each of the ways you are wasting your mental energy.

4. Learn the tools and habits to start incorporating these positive alternatives into your life.

Many people pay thousands of dollars for products and pills to relieve anxiety and depression which claim to be able to end all of X (where X may be fear, procrastination, or negative thinking). What they don't realize is that a great deal of good can come from natural tools, habits, a bit of awareness, and the slow, steady process of getting one's life together...

...And some work. Nothing good was ever spawned from doing no work, and everyone that says that you can be better without any work is lying to you. I will give you the tools, but you must go out and do the work. You must make an effort to incorporate these things into your life. If you take it seriously, you will be successful. If you don't take it seriously, then you won't move forward, and you will be stuck where you are right now.

There are no shortcuts here, sorry.

That doesn't mean you won't be able to celebrate little victories along the way though — make sure to eat some ice cream now and then...

This resource is here for you to learn these life-altering tools. This is the result of years of my reading through books, blog articles, and forums. From filling out 300-page work books. From sweat, tears, frustration, and hours and hours of dedicated work. I have tried many things and have discarded everything that was hurtful or absolutely useless.

Everything in this book I have tested myself, and would not include it otherwise. I do nearly each item that will be mentioned here every day, either subconsciously (I've integrated it into my life so that it's automatic), or consciously everyday.

It's time to unlock the power you have inside that can be clouded by negative habits. Stop procrastinating. Stop worrying. Stop looking at people with jealousy.

It's time to reclaim your mental energy.

Chapter 2.
Why Should You Listen to Me? - My (Shortened) Story

Check out the pictures below of these two guys. Notice any differences?

Actually, they are the same guy...

Me.

On the left is me before beginning my journey into self-improvement and on the right is me after three years of hard work and exploration. You can see that:

- I take A LOT better care of myself in terms of my appearance.

- I'm actually SMILING.

- In the old picture I look scared and tense. In the recent one I look happy and hopeful.

- My eyes shine brighter.

I used to desperately desire to connect with people. I had a great deal of shame, I was scared, and my mind beat me down. I didn't do anything about my situation, assuming nothing could ever change.

I suffered from a great deal of anxiety and depression that I didn't even know about, and still struggle with today. But despite that, I have done some amazing things in the past few years. I've:

1. Gone up to attractive women on the street that I've never met before, gotten their numbers, and gone on dates with them.

2. Traveled around Europe for three months, the majority of which was done completely solo.

3. Done meditation retreats, not talking to anyone for 10 days and meditating for over 10 hours a day.

4. Learned how to connect with people in minutes and get them to open up about deep emotions.

5. Had incredibly intimate relationships with women that I never thought possible before.

6. Started my own businesses.

7. Relocated to Vietnam.

As I worked on myself I had to do a GREAT deal of research and work to find tools that could help me accomplish these things. This book is intended to give you an overview of some of the things that have made me FAR happier in life, so that you too can go after what you want. You can stop being controlled by your mind.

Chapter 3.
Why Is It Important to Reclaim Your Mental Energy?

Do you ever hear yourself thinking:

"Why did this happen to me?"

"If only this could be different..."

"I feel like I'm going to fail..."

"Ooh, if this goes well I think that they'll like me..."

The problem is that these thoughts are aimed at either:

1. **Altering the past**

2. **Changing the present reality**

3. **Predicting the future**

   All of these tasks are actually impossible to do.

   You can't alter the past, as it has already happened.

   You can't change the current reality, you can only accept it and live with it while trying to make the brightest possible future for yourself (aligned with your goals, hopes, and dreams).

   You can't predict the future, because uh...you're not Madame Zorba.

   Once you realize that these three actions are futile, you can start focusing your energy on what is worth your time. For example:

You can learn from the past, instead of trying to alter it and wish that

9

it didn't happen, so you have a better present and future.

You can learn to be grateful for what you have right now and make an action plan to deal with a currently troubling situation, always moving forward.

You can accept that the future hasn't happened yet and that you can only plan and prepare so much. You can never predict everything.

Two important concepts come from this, which will be the cornerstone of this book and your learning. You must:

1. **Live in the present (and not the past or future).**

2. **Accept the present reality as it is, and not as you would like it to be.**

Chapter 4.
Defining Expectations - You Will Never Be Perfect

The point of this book is **NOT** to make you 100% perfect. You won't be an efficient robot—you're still human. I hate to tell you this, but **YOU WILL ALWAYS WASTE SOME MENTAL ENERGY**. And that's OK.

We are aiming for improvement, not perfection. Let's not get into a discussion about **perfectionism** right now—there's a chapter dedicated to that later...

After reading this book, you should be conscious of some of the ways you are wasting your energy, so you can slowly improve your life.

Chapter 5.
The Emotional and Logical Brains

Often you will hear people say that "they are of two minds." Sometimes, this refers to left and right brain thinking: Some people are more artistic and creative, and others are more logical and mathematical. But what is less commonly discussed is the split between **the logical and emotional brains**. This is essential to overcome any mental waste.

Your **emotional brain** is more child-like, and is where all your feelings come from. If you feel anxious and that results in a burning in your chest, it's your emotional brain reacting to something. If you feel happy, it's coming from your emotional brain.

So what's the problem? Emotions can be great! But, when you get really involved in an emotion or you feel like the world will collapse, the **logical brain** is absolutely essential to becoming grounded again and moving forward in life.

Think of the logical brain as the parent to the child-like emotional brain, helping it through whatever it's going through. You don't rain on its parade, but you help it if it's in trouble or needs to be reeled in. You use your logical brain to talk yourself into moving forward despite emotional reactions, being OK with negative emotions, or knowing that really intense emotions won't last forever.

A lot of the time, for emotions like fear, we FEEL as if we're going to die if we do something (your emotional brain is reacting), but logically we could reason out that we would be OK if we do the thing, and something great might actually come from it. For example, if someone has a lot of social anxiety, talking to someone might feel like the hardest thing in the world, and seem very dangerous. But, if they use their logical brain to tell themselves..."Hey, I've talked to people before and survived. How likely is it that a conversation will really kill me? I mean, there's like a 0.0001% that a conversation can result in death. And I ride my bike to work ever day... Riding a bike is technically more dangerous because I might get hit by a car, yet I do that and I'm totally fine! This really isn't a big deal"...they can probably move forward.

Being able to use the logical brain to talk to the emotional one is especially important for those with an overactive **amygdala**.

What the heck is that? Don't worry, there are no crazy biology lessons here. What you should know is that research has shown that our memories are stored in the amygdala. It is a section of the brain important in processing decision-making, memory, and emotional reactions. Unfortunately, those who have undergone traumatic experiences in childhood (social outcasting, bullying, abuse, etc....) will have their emotional brains fire off at the flick of a switch. Someone changing lanes in a car may take caution to make sure that they don't hit anyone. But someone with an overactive amygdala starts sweating and worrying, and their adrenaline starts pumping just with a simple lane switch.

You will see that the mental wastes we analyze usually stem from the emotional side of the brain, and the exercises we do come from the logical brain explaining what will happen. A lot of the tools you will learn about in this book involve using your logical brain to talk to your emotional one.

You will learn that you can't let emotions control you. You can and NEED to feel all of them, but you can control how you react. Much of this book will teach you how to stop automatically reacting to everything and everyone. Just because you feel an emotion doesn't mean you have to react in the first way you feel (e.g., extreme anger leading to knocking someone's block off, or jealousy leading to over-texting and manipulation).

In other words, one cannot control fear, but one sure as hell doesn't have to be controlled by it. If that were the case, I can assure you I would have never have said hello to one girl in my life.

And that doesn't sound too fun to me.

So, how do we begin to hear our emotional brain? What are we going to learn together?

Chapter 6.
What You Are Going to Learn

In this book, I will guide you as you learn exactly how you are wasting your mental energy. As we move through the tenses (past, future, and present), I will highlight types of thoughts related to each and how they are zapping your mental energy. Specifically, each will be broken down to explain what it is, why it's bad, and how you can help yourself. You'll also learn exercises so you can actually apply this in real life!

Ensure that you at least read all the way through the book to before the Mental Waste Catalog before skipping around! If you don't have a problem with a specific mental waste, go ahead and skip the section dedicated to it. But, I encourage you to read as much as you can because there might be something you aren't aware of that is severely handicapping you in life.

You might be saying, "But Noam, I can't hear any of my thoughts, I don't know what's going on." Or maybe you're a bit murky on your internal workings.

That's OK. The first tool you will learn will help you hear what is going on inside your head, and help promote a more peaceful life.

The key to having more mental energy NOW is that you will learn many little techniques and habits that together will drive you forward. There's no magic pill that will make you never waste any energy, but there are a lot of little things that can add up to a HUGE difference.

While you will learn about many mental wastes and methods of significantly decreasing them, there is a reoccurring theme in this book. If you take nothing else, remember:

Life is not lived in the mind, it is lived in physical reality. Most mental wastes deal with refusing to accept the present. Learn to accept the present by controlling your reactions and dealing with it in a positive and mature fashion, and you will be far happier.

Deal with the mental waste, but then snap back to the present. The past and future live in our minds—the present is the only thing that actually exists.

Your default state of living should be in the present, and you should only go into your mind for brief periods. If you are ever in doubt, come back to the present.

"*Be present.*" That sounds familiar. But what exactly is "being present," and how do you do it?

Section II

Mental Energy Theory, Mindfulness, and Meditation

Chapter 7.
An Introduction to Mindfulness and The Law of Nature

Before getting into the mental wastes themselves, we need to ensure that you can hear your thoughts well. Some people will be better at this than others.

Chances are that if you are reading this book, this isn't your first foray into self-improvement literature. But if it is, welcome! Either way, you've probably heard of things like "*mindfulness*" or "*being present*" before.

But what exactly does this mean?

In general, being present means you do not look into the future for what might happen (good or bad). You do not live in the past and wish it was different, or that you could re-live it. You live in the singular moment being experienced right now—all the good, bad, or whatever is going on. And, you accept it as it is, and **NOT** as you would like it to be.

It is quite easy to wave a hand and say, "Yes, yes. I accept things, I'm here," but are you really?

When something bad happens, do you smile and say, "Well, I know I was happy before, and I can't be sad forever, so I'll just let this go," or do you get grumpy, wish it didn't happen, and berate yourself?

The **Law of Nature**, a principle from Buddhism, says that everything arises just to pass away. Everything. Thoughts, emotions, objects, and even you. You will eventually die one day, and that's OK (hopefully you knew that...unless you're superhuman and defy time.

In which case, call me).

So first, this knowledge of everything arising just to pass away should give you some peace of mind to know that bad times won't last forever, and neither will bad moods. The only way they will last forever is if you PUSH THEM AWAY, REJECT THEM, or in other words...REFUSE TO ACCEPT THEM.

All those guys that are "being present" are so peaceful, because they don't fight reality. It's not that bad things don't happen to them— they just don't fight them when they do. And when good things happen they enjoy them fully, but also know that they can't last forever (so they aren't depressed when they disappear).

This first piece of information should help you free up some mental energy. Don't worry, we'll get into how to "become present" in a bit.

Chapter 8.
Applying The Law of Nature to Your Thoughts

This book is specifically focused on mental energy and thoughts, so let's examine those topics with regards to the **Law of Nature**.

If everything arises just to pass away, then so must your thoughts. **The problem is that over the course of your life you have been trained (whether you realized it or not) to react to certain thoughts stemming from certain situations**. But not everyone reacts the same way.

Take for example the case of two good guy friends: One studies really hard and is amazing at school, but is not the best at socializing. The other is a social dynamo, and while he wants to do well in school, never really grasps the concepts.

The book-smart guy, **Booky**, gets a bit nervous for exams but knows he'll do awesome, so he isn't that worried. He hears small thoughts like, "*Oh man, I might bomb this!*" but ignores them because he knows it always turns out well.

The socially savvy guy, **Savvy**, gets a bit nervous when going on dates with girls. "*Ahh, it's always so awkward doing stuff like this, when do I go in for the kiss? Oh well, I know I'll eventually kiss her either way.*" He's done it before and he knows people generally like him, so he usually does fine and the girls like him.

Now when the two guys swap places they can't control their thoughts: Booky is in full-blown anxiety mode if he has a date. He feels scared. He doesn't have a lot of experience. He can't really say he knows it will turn out well. Same with Savvy when he has a test, especially since he never does well on tests, no matter what!

Booky reacts with anxiety to social situations.

Savvy reacts with anxiety to testing in school.

Same feeling, different situation. And they complain about it.

Of course both could do better in either situation by exposing themselves (Booky by going on more low-key dates to start, Savvy by doing extra hours of school). But we'll leave that to when we get into the mental wastes.

When you are in certain situations or dealing with things, you will have thoughts come and go. Sometimes, thoughts can just fly away (like Booky with bombing a test). Others will continually circle and beat you down!

In reading this book you will learn how to change your thought processes to focus on ones that fuel your energy and give you positivity.

You will accept negative thoughts and use them to point you to items you should take care of (using them to motivate you to take action instead of ruminating on them).

But at the end of everything, you will need to come back to the present moment in front of you. Our goal is to free you from the chains that are keeping you down, but not to keep you inside the mind where everything seems to be all nice after this work.

Your mind will always spit out negative thoughts—you just learn to ignore them.

You still need to do your living in the "real world."

Chapter 9.
Mental Energy Theory and Thinking Patterns

"You're telling me to ignore my negative thoughts?"

You may have more than 50,000 thoughts each day[1]. Some are positive, some are negative, and some are neutral. Depending on what you have been through as a person, the proportions may change.

As we discussed in the last chapter, some people react to different situations or thoughts quite differently. Many of us will cling to negative, fear-induced thoughts while ignoring the positive ones. This causes people to become stuck in negativity and travel down ever-darker paths.

I can tell you that while writing this book I had many thoughts like *"This is a waste of time,"* *"You don't even know if people will like it,"* and *"You're going to fail."* But, they only stick out in my mind and have weight if I give them lots of my energy. That's what would lead to me feeling negative emotions. Remember: **What you think is what you feel**. But I also hear thoughts like, *"This is going to help people"* and *"You're doing something most people can't do."* Most people give far too much weight to any thought they have, and that causes their moods to change very quickly. Take this example of how multiple thoughts crop up when something happens:

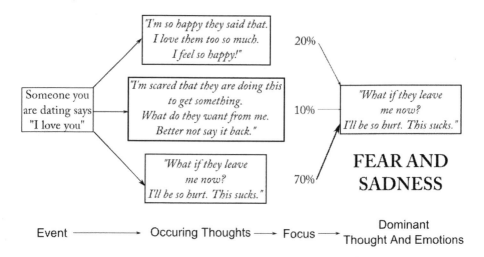

Someone saying "*I love you*" causes a person to hear multiple thoughts. But because of their psychological makeup and past, they choose to focus on how much it might hurt if the person leaves them, and that this situation sucks. This is a major cause of depression! Another person in a different situation might acknowledge that it would hurt if the person left, but be INCREDIBLY happy and grateful for having someone that loves them.

Can you see how important this is and how much of a difference it can make in your life? Are you aware of some patterns that you might have?

You will hear many thoughts throughout the day in reaction to many events—getting up, being late for work, someone saying "*I love you*"... The work you will begin is to hear every thought, negative or positive, but then consciously focus on the positive ones and disregard those that are negative. This does not mean that you push negative thoughts down—you just hear them and let them go.

Brilliant, strong people are not formed by everything going well in their lives—they are built by both bad and good things happening, and reacting in a positive or constructive way no matter what.

As you might have guessed, you're going to learn later, by going through each mental waste chapter, about how to get on a positive wavelength more frequently with different techniques.

The Thinking and Observing Minds

This all relates to a topic based in Eastern philosophy on the **thinking and observing minds**. If you are hearing yourself think, then it follows that you can't be exactly what you think. Mark Manson summarized the difference between the two in one of his articles.[2]

To paraphrase, if I tell you not to think of a pink elephant—WHATEVER YOU DO, NO THINKING OF PINK ELEPHANTS—it's too late, you probably thought of a bunch. Aww...they look so cute!

You see, we cannot control the thoughts that come, or the actions of our thinking minds. We will see many thoughts throughout the day.

All we can control is our reaction to our thoughts—in other words, how much we believe or focus on them.

What is important—as a basis for the rest of this book—and what I want you to remember is that whatever you give energy to will grow in your mind.

Think of the thoughts like little plants, and you thinking on them is giving those plants sunlight and water. If you don't give those plants sunlight and water, they can't grow.[3]

Guess which thoughts I'd rather have grow and flourish in my mind?

Let me get a bit nerdy for a second and refer to this as **Mental Energy Theory**. The fundamental law to remember: **The Law of Mental Energy** says that:

THE ENERGY YOU GIVE TO SPECIFIC THOUGHTS DETERMINES YOUR MOOD, EMOTIONS, SELF-ESTEEM, REALITY, AND CONFIDENCE.

So **be careful**.

Your mind can trick you as well. You might hear *"This book is a waste of time, I should stop reading it."*

Well, please don't do that because there is a lot to learn about helping yourself! But this is just your mind coming up with a thought. I'm sure you picked up this book for a reason. You want to learn how to be happier and waste less mental energy. So you are going to disregard that thought and tell yourself *"I know this is worth it, I'm doing this to make myself better and happier,"* and keep on going.

With all this being said, let's move on to learning meditation techniques to help you observe your thoughts so you can find out if and when negative thoughts arise. And also, to practice not reacting to these thoughts.

---

[1] Davis, Bruce. *There Are 50,000 Thoughts Standing Between You and Your Partner Every Day!* Huffington Post. Retrieved from http://www.huffingtonpost.com/bruce-davis-phd/healthy-relationships_b_3307916.html on October 2nd, 2014.

[2] Manson, Mark. *Your Two Minds.* markmanson.net. Retrieved from http://markmanson.net/your-two-minds on January 7th, 2015.

[3] While this has been discussed by many and framed in different ways, the earliest mention of it that I've ever read came from an essay by James Allen, published in 1902. It is an excellent read and available for free at: http://www.asamanthinketh.net/.

Chapter 10.
Basic Anapana Meditation for Thought Observation

The meditation this book will teach you is known as Anapana, as given by the Vipassana meditation tradition.[1] To really go into the depths of meditation and get A LOT out of it, I highly recommend you go on one of their 10-day retreats, which are completely free of charge. I have attended two of these (as of writing of this book) and plan to do one every year because I have found them to be so cleansing and beneficial. Moreover, the full technique of Vipassana is only allowed to be taught by learned mentors. You can read more about the benefits of going on a retreat here.[2]

What I will be explaining is also known as mindfulness meditation.

Here are the steps to begin practicing Anapana meditation:

1. Begin by being in a quiet place. Dim the lights.

2. Sit comfortably. If you have glasses, take them off. You do not have to sit in a lotus or scrunched up yogi position. You can even sit in a chair if that's more comfortable. Just be relaxed, and try to keep your back straight.

3. Close your eyes.

4. Begin by simply being where you are, and breathing. Breathe through your nose only, not your mouth. Keep your mouth closed.

5. If you've never done meditation, this is going to be EXTREMELY challenging. You will probably start thinking

things like *"This is a waste of time," "I'm not doing this right, let me go research how to do meditation,"* etc. Welcome to the first stages of observing your thoughts and NOT REACTING.

6. You goal is to feel the flow of breath coming in and out of your nose. Your can feel it inside the nostrils, at the base of them... It doesn't matter where you feel it, just feel the breath. Do **NOT** try to make the breath faster or slower. Learning to accept reality as it is (and not reacting by trying to change things) starts with your breath.

Pretty simple, right?

Simple to learn, difficult to practice.

Aim to get up to at least 30 minutes per day of this for some real benefits. The more the better. As a side benefit, you'll find yourself feeling more relaxed and able to handle life's problems because you are inherently observing the reality of your thoughts, and not trying to stop them or control them.

Start with just trying to do one minute. Then try five. Then 10. And keep building it up slowly everyday. It will take patience, but it's worth it! Try and do it at the same time everyday (e.g., before leaving for work, before bed, etc.).

You may get in your head a lot and have a hard time staying present. That's OK! As Dr. Robert Glover said: "You will lose consciousness a million times a day, just make sure you re-gain it a million and one."

---

[1] For more information or to learn about going on a FREE retreat, see: http://www.dhamma.org/.

[2] See: http://lightwayofthinking.com/7-benefits-going-vipassana-meditation-retreat/ .

Chapter 11.
I'm Accepting Thoughts, Yet Later We're Changing Them?

You might be confused because I said we would be changing your thoughts to get them to be less wasteful.

Yes and no.

Again, because you can't control your thinking mind-you can't control your thoughts, ever. But, as you learned with The Law of Mental Energy, you can control which ones you listen to and focus on —which ones you water in your "mind garden." And moreover, you can PUT IN your own thoughts through positive self-talk, which is what we will be doing throughout the course of this book.

Now that you have an idea of how to observe your thoughts— how you can't control them, but you can control which ones you focus on—it is time to begin examining the different mental wastes and how to stop them.

Section III

Mental Waste Catalog, Overview, and Action Plan

Chapter 12.
How Each Mental Waste Will Be Explained

As a brief reminder from the introduction, each mental waste chapter will be broken down as such:

- Description.

- Why you might do it and where it comes from-why it's bad and useless to you.

- What is the positive alternative that will boost our mental energy, and how it can help you.

- Practical exercises and tools to help you incorporate the positive alternative into your life, and get rid of or minimize the waste.

Chapter 13.
An Overview of the Mental Wastes

Here is a breakdown of the mental wastes you will learn how to beat in this book, separated into tenses—past, present, and future. The breakdown is done in a way such that each waste would be something you associate with a certain tense. For example, you usually worry about the future, and regret something in your past:

Past

- *Regret* – Feeling sad that you missed out on or didn't do something. Feeling bad about a decision you made.

- *Remembering* – Continuously living in the past and "good times." Refusing to move on.

-

Future

- *Projection, Fortune Telling, and Fantasy* – Trying to predict what will happen, day dreaming, thinking about how bad an event could be.

- *Fear* – The general state of feeling scared when attempting to do something. Or, refusing to do something at all because of the troublesome feelings.

- *Anxiety and Worry* – Predicting negative outcomes in the future and a general state of negative thinking.

Present

- *Complaining* – Thinking things SHOULD be different. Refusing to accept what is in front of you, instead of taking action to change things if possible.

- *Excuses* – Making reasons why you can't or won't do something.

- *Churning and Spiraling* – Continuously multiplying your thoughts, staying stuck in your head, ruminating.

- *Trying to Remember Everything* – Thinking that you can keep everything organized in your head, leading to excessive stress, and forgetting important items.

- *Jealousy and Envy* – Feeling anger or hatred towards someone who has something that you want but haven't obtained yet.

- *Perfectionism* – Thinking something has to be PERFECT and refusing to move on, take action, or release or do something until that thing is up to an arbitrary (unattainable) standard.

- *Procrastination* – The act of filling time with busy work or time-wasting activities instead of doing what needs to be done.

- *Self-Criticism and Negative Self-Talk* – Talking harshly to yourself and being self-critical, finding flaws about yourself no matter what. Assuming you will always screw up and fail.

- *Blame* – When something goes wrong, moving the fault to anyone but yourself.

- *Pessimism, Negative Thinking, and Limiting Beliefs* – Always assuming and focusing on the negative in a situation. Being chained down by beliefs in the world that do not serve you.

- *Guessing What Someone Is Thinking About You and Trying to Please Others* – Assuming you can predict how someone feels about you and trying to do everything to make others happy, even if it is at the cost of your own needs.

- *Assuming the Present Will Never Change and Over-Identifying with It* – Becoming extremely sensitive to acute emotions or events in the present and making a huge fuss, versus knowing that all things will end and change.

- *Comparing Yourself to Others* – The act of comparing your physical or mental attributes, life events, or possessions to that of someone else.

- *Rushing* – Moving from one thing to the next either in work, relationships, events, and in general, in life, without stopping or being able to appreciate what is in front of you.

Remember, the point is not to be **perfect**—that's impossible. You can never eliminate your thought wastes 100%. But, you can become aware of how you shoot yourself in the foot, learn positive ways to talk to yourself, and significantly relieve yourself of useless stress, anxiety, and sadness.

Chapter 14.
How to Progress Through the Book

With so many of these wastes, you might be asking if you should try to read everything through right away. I don't recommend that. The point is that you are supposed to learn about these wastes and how they hurt you, but then **DO THE EXERCISES**. Take it from an over-planner who used reading as an excuse for running from action, challenging situations, and change: **THE EXERCISES ARE THE MOST IMPORTANT PART OF THIS BOOK AND YOUR WORK**.

You will not change just by reading.

I suggest you proceed in one of two ways:

1. Take a quick look through the table of contents in the mental waste catalog section or at the breakdown of the mental wastes in the last section. If you see something that strikes you as being something that you might have a problem with ("Oh, I'm really bad at **worrying**"), then you can read the description of that waste and see if you should tackle it.

2. If you just have a general interest in how you can reclaim any mental energy, read through the wastes one at a time and do each exercise if you think it could help you.

PATIENCE is the name of the game. Each exercise will be done almost everyday for a period of time. You need a longer period of time for them to take any effect. Just doing them once will give you a bit of a placebo effect, but the point is to make a LASTING change.

Whatever you choose to do, only tackle **ONE** or **TWO** mental waste exercises at a time. Overloading yourself will also be counterproductive. Focus to stay sane and be happy.

If you read this book front to back, you will notice that there is some repetition of content and cross-referencing between sections. I have structured this book so that if you were to read one section on a specific mental waste you are having issues with—such as **complaining**—it would be self-contained. While I may refer to different chapters for your reference, you can read that one chapter by itself and know what you need to help you with that mental waste.

Chapter 15.
A Plan for the Exercises

As you begin reading about the mental wastes, you will see that at the end of each Chapter (or mental waste), there are exercises, tools, or habits to implement in your life that will work to get rid of the waste. You might feel stuck, wondering how long you should spend with each waste and exercise. Unfortunately, every person will be different. Everyone takes a different amount of time to instill habits depending on their psychology, strengths, and weaknesses.

The important thing is to really focus on **one or two** of the tools at a time in the **SAME** waste section. Don't mix them (unless a section contains a reference to another exercise in a different section).

However, I have outlined the tools and wastes here with an approximate timeline to at least give you a starting idea of how long I think you should spend on each. And yes, the total time adds up to A LOT. That's because you are trying to instill lifelong habits. This is not a quick fix, though one or two tools can make a HUGE difference.

BUT FIRST:

Begin regular journaling and meditation for **two weeks**, done every day, once a day, at approximately the same time. However, they do not have to be done together – I meditate in the morning and journal at night.

Then you can move on to the mental wastes. The names won't make too much sense right now, but come back once you've read a Chapter and are wondering about the time to spend:

The Past

1. Regret

- *Regret Journalling* - 3 days.

- *Ladder Method For Conquering Fear (Progressive Desensitization)* - I suggest at least 5-6 steps, but depends on the fear you are working on. Each should be done on sequential days, so 5-6 days.

- *Fear Journal* - All throughout life.

2. Remembering

- *Using The Past To Fuel The Future* - Once an event has happened - 1 week. Otherwise, use in the moment as needed.

- *You Can't Run From Pain* - Once an event has happened - 1 week. Otherwise, use in the moment as needed.

The Future

3. Projection/Fortune Telling And Fantasy

- *Negative To Positive Projection* - 2 weeks.

- *Fantasy And Positive Projection – Use It To Manifest Your Dreams!* - 3 days.

4. Fear

See **Regret.**

5. Anxiety/Worry

- *Talking To Others* - Make a conscious effort for 2 weeks to talk to someone every time you feel fear. If not in the moment, then the same day.

- *Positive And Supportive Self-Improvement-Talk* - 2 weeks.

- *5 Minutes Of Space* - Give yourself this time when necessary over the next month.

- *20 Minute Buffer* - Implement into your scheduled appointments TODAY. Keep this for a month.

6. Assuming Nothing Will Ever Change

Follow steps as laid out in chapter when needed - 2 weeks.

The Present

7. Complaining

- *No Complaint Experiment* - 3 weeks.

8. Excuses

N/A.

9. Churning And Spiraling

- *Do It Now Or Drop It* - 2 weeks.

- *Will This Matter In X Time* - 3 weeks.

- *Re-direction* - 2 weeks.

10. Trying To Remember Everything

- *Calendar* - Create your calendar, try using it for a month.

- *Notebooks* - Buy a bunch of notebooks to use for work, while walking around, beside your bed... Try writing in them for a month and see how you feel.

- *Evernote* - Implement immediately and dump everything into the notes here. Use it for 2 weeks at least.

- *Text Yourself* - Whenever needed!

11. Jealousy And Envy

- *Gratitude Exercise And Practice* - 3 weeks.

- *Why Am I Jealous And What Am I Going To Do About It?* - Try for the next week.

12. Perfectionism

- *Positive Self-Talk About Yourself And Others* - 1 month.

13. Procrastination

N/A.

14. Self-Criticism And Negative Self-Talk

- *I Am My Own Best Friend* - 3 weeks.

- *Doing Things For Myself* - 3 weeks.

- *Taking Compliments Fully And Compliments Document* - 2 weeks.

15. Blame

N/A.

16. Pessimism And Negative Thinking

- *Biofeedback And The Rubber Band* - 3 weeks.

- *Replace Negative Thoughts With Positive Variants* - 2 weeks.

- *De-programming Limiting Beliefs* - Depends on the belief, but at least 2 weeks of conscious effort is required.

- *Catch And Release* - 1 month.

Chapter 15. A Plan for the Exercises

17. Guessing What Someone Else Is Thinking About You/ Trying To Please Others

- *Bucket List* - Do it now. Work on it for the rest of your life, and re-visit it every time you think of something else you'd love to do.

- *Take Notice And Sooth* - 2 weeks.

18. Assuming The Present Will Never Change And Over-Identifying With It

- *Feeling Your Emotions* - 1 week.

- *Unsticking Negativity By Expanding Your Scope* - 3 weeks.

19. Comparing Yourself To Others

N/A.

20. Rushing

- *This Is Important Now* - 2 weeks.

- *3 Things Today* - 2 weeks.

- *Scheduling Stops* - 2 weeks.

- *1 Day Off* - For the rest of your life except in extreme circumstances.

- *What Is Important To Me* - Do it now. Re-do it at least every year. Then work towards eliminating the crappy activities!

Chapter 16.
The Importance of Journaling and Accountability

Before finally getting into the mental wastes there are two last things you need to be aware of: **journaling** and **accountability**.

Journaling

While learning, reading, and all of that is important, you need to be tracking things to actually SEE what is happening. What thoughts are coming up? How do you feel? Are you surprised at how much energy you waste?

That's why nearly every exercise incorporates a journaling portion. Do NOT skip this—it is important to see the changes that are happening. You'll also be able to review all the progress you've made in case you have a down day!

Begin keeping a journal NOW and write down how you feel throughout the day, what happened, and your progression on the exercises. Each exercise will have specific instructions of what to journal, but you should be journaling almost every night to track your life and for reflection and introspection on your journey.

Accountability

If you are serious about reclaiming your mind, you need to take all the necessary steps you can to ensure that the work is being done.

If you are having trouble getting the exercises done, I suggest you also implement steps to hold yourself accountable. Sometimes our minds want to sabotage us or we just feel too lazy to do something important—but then, you will never move forward or improve if you allow that.

There are two ways to move forward with accountability—personally (by yourself) or with a partner.

1. **Personal** - Set up a simple spreadsheet with the exercise you are trying to accomplish and dates of the year (January 1, January 2, etc.). Every night, you need to check off that you did this exercise. If you have, you get a reward (watch your favorite TV show, healthy snack, video games, whatever). If you don't, you can either just not get the reward, or you might get punished as well (have to pay someone money, not get to go out on the weekend, etc.). A combination of both might work as well, but there needs to be an external force making you want to or not want to do this. Hence the reward and/or punishment.

2. **Partner** - You need to call or text a partner every week or possibly every day to let them know how you did. It will be between you two to decide what happens if you slip up on several days. But the point here is that you have to report to someone, and you aren't just leaving it to your own means to move forward. For example, if you missed one day on your exercises, you pay them $20. Now that someone outside wants to collect from you, it's even MORE of a push to get your stuff done.

Remember: Success = effort. I can give you the exercises, but you need to do them. Reading won't get you far—it's just an introduction. You need to go out and also write about what happened.

Let's get started.

Section IV

Mental Wastes of the Past

Chapter 17.
Regret

"I'll never get a chance to do that again. I wish I had taken that opportunity."

Because of fear, bad circumstances, or just choosing one activity over another, you create regret. When you have that feeling that you missed out on something for some reason, you feel it in the pit of your stomach. You promise yourself you'll never miss out again, but then it keeps recurring. Why?

Why You Might Do It and Where It Comes From

Regret can be mind nonsense. For example, you might choose one activity over another. That's a conscious choice you must live with, and you need to ask, every moment, what's best for you. Sure, you could go to the party when you are sick, but is that really what you should be doing? Sometimes you can't do everything you want for external reasons beyond your control, and that's OK. That is part of accepting reality as it is (harder than accepting being in an amazing mood, right?).

Bigger issues come when you don't do something because of **fear**. Your fear might hold you back from doing something challenging or scary, and that IS in your control. Not the emotion—fear is normal—but your ability and skill to push through and do the scary thing anyways. You can feel scared about talking to someone or going on a trip, but if you give in to fear, you will be controlled by it for the rest of your life.

What's the Positive Alternative to Boost Your Mental Energy?

In this sense, regret often makes you feel bad for no reason (external reasons beyond your control), and you need to let go. You need to accept that you can't be a billion places at once, and you need to decide on your priorities. For example, with the party, it would be valuing our health and livelihood over seeing your friends, at least in that moment. There will be a time for friends again once you are better.

If there's something you really want to do on a weekday but you have work, then you can either shift the hours to another day, or accept that maybe you need to consider getting a more flexible job if you aren't allowed.

Sometimes, when combined with **self-criticism**, you chastise yourself for not doing something in the moment that you wanted to do. If it's due to fear, you can work on that. If it's due to other obligations, you need to accept that you have limitations and can't do everything. If it's because you think you should have done something else in that moment, or could have, you're driving yourself nuts for no reason and missing out on all the amazing things you had then and there. You should drop that thought entirely.

So you can actually spin regret in a positive fashion—you can use it to show yourself how to move towards your ideal life (e.g., more flexible job), and also what you need to work on (in terms of fears you want to get over).

Practical Exercises

Letting go and accepting that we have priorities is a lifelong process, as are the subtleties of job flexibility. Let's focus on the fears.

For the **next three days**, you are going to record in a journal when you felt regret at the end of the day. The more you can write the better, since it will show you if there are some recurring patterns.

Look at the journal—what came up? Did you feel regret a lot when you couldn't talk to people you wanted to meet? Did you feel bad when you weren't assertive and didn't speak up for yourself?

Then, unfortunately, the only way out is through. You have to do the exact thing that scares you. This is the only way out of regret due to fear. Once you start doing things that are holding you back, there is no regret, because you are living the life you want free of fear.

Pick one fear and tackle it. If you find that this helps, you can move on to the other fears later.

If you have issues tackling the fear itself, you need to "step" yourself up to the fear. What I mean by that is progressively desensitizing yourself. This is a very common technique from cognitive behavioral therapy that helps alleviate anxiety. You do the easiest thing in the category of what you are trying to do, and then slowly work your way up to the "scariest" thing.

In doing these steps, slowly but surely, you build your confidence to the point where the ultimate thing you want to do doesn't seem as bad anymore. And, you're riding on a wave of confidence, to boot.

For example, if you are afraid of telling someone they are cute, do each of the following on sequential days to 20 different people:

- First, start with trying to just ask someone for the time.

- Then for directions.

- Then ask them how their day is going.

- Then compliment them on a piece of clothing you like on them.

- Then tell them they are cute.

- Then tell them they are cute and ask them out on a date or for their phone number.

The above is the dating ladder technique described by Mark Manson in his book *Models*.[1]

You could apply this to another area though. Say you would eventually like to be playing live music shows in front of audiences, but you feel too scared. First, start by recording yourself and showing it to a good friend. Then play live in front of that friend. Then two friends. Then to those friends and one each of their friends you don't know.

I think you get the picture by now. Step by step you work your way up to what you eventually want to do. Even if it takes a while, it's better than being held back forever in life. You just need to come up with the steps yourself—not expect yourself to do the hardest thing first—and be kind to yourself if you are having issues (in which case, break things down even further).

Journaling and Accountability

The main thing to track in the journal is if you have done your action step each day. That's simple. What will REALLY add some weight though is creating a table in your journal, with two columns having the labels "What I Thought Would Happen" and "What Actually Happened." This will show you that whatever you feared probably was far removed from what actually happened (even if it didn't go exactly as you wanted it to). You can also write down how you feel about the difference in imagined vs. actual realities.

I guarantee that when you go up and tell a girl she's cute (if you aren't doing it for reasons other than actually wanting to get to know her and see where things go), she'll smile and say thanks. You won't spontaneously combust—though I had a long period where I expected that to happen...

What I Thought Would Happen	What Actually Happened	My Thoughts on the Differences

Another thing you can do is to create a "**Conquering Fear Journal.**" Here, you can record all the information you filled out in the table above, every time you conquer a fear. Whenever you feel down or like you aren't succeeding in life, look at how many fears you've conquered and how you've grown as a person. This will help get you back on the positive and right path. It also shows you that, no matter what, you never die when you face fears...unless they involve physical altercations. This book does not suggest you begin street fighting—I'm trying to reduce your stress!

You can't let fear cause you to miss out on doing what you want to do, leading to a life full of regret.

A life lived in regret is not a life—it is a curse. Get serious, and start going after what you want, step by step!

---

[1] One of the books that formed a cornerstone of my life changes over the past few years. This is the main "dating" book I would recommend that men read if they are struggling with women.

Chapter 18.
Remembering

"I remember when I went there with her. I miss her so much."

There's nothing wrong with remembering some good memories of the past. I mean, memories are amazing because they can never die—hence, all the new research about events and experiences leading to far increased happiness compared to buying more material possessions. Possessions pass away and we can always buy more, or upgrade them (a topic I could write another short book on). There's also remembering people who have passed away (in terms of their legacy), or good times you had in a past relationship...

The problem is when you **LIVE** in these good memories. You refuse to let go of what happened, hoping for it again. You can't live without it happening again, and do not want to let go. Days and weeks go by...

Why You Might Do It and Where It Comes From

Usually this is your mind refusing to let go of something or someone. You either believe something like the memory will never happen again (e.g., times you spent with a significant other you just broke up with—you'll never find someone else), or your brain might be chastising you for not being present enough DURING the memories, and you feel regret. Or, you refuse to deal with the pain NOW of not being in the memory anymore, so you retreat to enjoying the happy times of the good memory.

54

What's the Positive Alternative to Boost Your Mental Energy?

The past is gone. You can't get it back, and you need to accept that. What you can do, however, is use the memories of the past to fuel you.

- Depressed and sad a relationship is finished? Remember how amazing it was, and use it as fire to find other amazing relationship. There are many people who you can be with, and though no one is the same and no one will replace who you were with, who knows who else you'll meet and what you'll do with them? One thing is for sure: Stressing and crying over what is gone will not get you out there making more beautiful connections or relationships.

- Missing an event or trip? Use the amazing times you had as fuel to get your ass to another similar event or to save up for another trip.

When I broke up with my first "real" (non-high school) girlfriend in my 20s, I stressed and cried that I would never find anyone else. I agonized over the break-up decision for hours before doing it because, though there were problems between us, I didn't want to let go of the emotions we had. Breaking up was the right thing to do though, and as time went on I met other girls who I had even deeper connections with. The memories I had with each person are irreplaceable, but now anytime something ends I use it as fuel to find other people to connect with. Things just keep getting better and better as I proceed through life.

Practical Exercises

Remember the **Law of Nature**. One of the fundamental laws of Buddhism is that all things arise just to pass away. Events, people, relationships...they all will eventually end and cease to exist. Even the best married relationships eventually end when one partner passes away. If you can keep this concept front and center in your mind, you won't be as sad when things end, because you know they cannot last forever. You will make the most and enjoy things as much as you can now, but not cling to them when they stop. Don't get into the negative mindset of *"Well if things will end, what's the point?"* The fact is that things will end, that's OK, and another event will come if you are open to it. Another person will come as well. A bad mood will go and a happy mood will come again.

Stop stressing.

There are two things you need to focus on if you have issues with **remembering**, or just can't seem to stop living in the past:

• ## Using the Past to Fuel the Future

Re-frame the memories, as the positive alternative section says: Anytime you hear yourself saying or thinking *"I miss X," "I wish it was the way it was,"* or *"Will it ever be the same?"* think about fueling yourself to find another event or activity. This is not to replace the memory. Treasure the memory as something unique and special. Rather, it is to know that more events and memories will come.

• ## You Can't Run from Pain

You may be running from pain. You might be living in the past to avoid dealing with a difficult situation now. This is especially the case if you have ended a significant relationship. Remembering is a natural part of grieving, but **DON'T BEAT YOURSELF UP HERE.** The problem arises when you spend days or weeks there.

Bring your attention now with the meditation instructions in this book (see Chapter 10). Close your eyes and feel your breath. Do you start feeling a choking in your neck, tightness in your chest, or pain in your head?

That's OK. Feel that. It's not going to feel good, but you can't run from what you feel now. You need to embrace that and be OK with the uncomfortable feelings.

If it is too difficult to do this alone, you may need to add an additional action step of going to talk to someone—either a friend or a trained therapist who can help you move into the present, or to deal with the difficult emotions.

Journaling and Accountability

Write down at least one time every day when you hear your mind trying to re-live the past, and how you re-framed it to fuel yourself into the future. How did that change your feelings? What do you think you should do now to create more memories or find more people? What's the smallest step you can take? Is it putting one cent into savings, looking up meetup.com events, etc.?

OR

Write down at least one time every day when you felt bad sensations (like you were being choked, or felt like crying), or bad feelings. Why do you think they are there? How long did they last?

As an overall mindset, keep this close to you, forever and always:

Don't be sad it's over, be grateful that it happened.

Section V

Mental Wastes of the Future

Chapter 19.
Projection, Fortune Telling, and Fantasy

"Ahh, if I take that job overseas I'm going to starve!"
"Oh God I can imagine him taking me in his arms..."

These mental wastes are closely related.

The first, **projection** or **fortune telling**, is when you assume that you know exactly what will happen in the future and can predict it. This can be somewhat positive ("Oh, I know I'll get that raise so I can buy the car now! No worries!") or negative ("She won't like me, why bother.") We can call each **positive** and **negative projection**, respectively.

The second, **fantasy**, projects into the future but is a large over-exaggeration of a positive outcome and "what things could be like." For instance, living on an exotic island, how sex with someone would be like, and so on.

As usual, doing any of these a bit is natural: When faced with a decision, you will look to the future to see if something could be a bad choice. When you are dating someone, OF COURSE you might think about what sex would be like with them. Or, when you are working towards a certain lifestyle, you might imagine how it would be when you succeed.

The issue is when these take over, or when you project so much that reality does not align with your imagined state and you become frustrated. Take, for example, when you imagined how sex would be with someone—but it was far different, in a bad way, and you became irritated. Or, when a lifestyle wasn't all it was cracked up to be. This just leads to anger.

Why You Might Do It and Where It Comes From

Living in the future can come from two things:

1. **Fear of the unknown** - You don't know what's going to happen, and you feel scared. So you either project something bad occurring to keep yourself from even trying (that's no good at all) or you project something good happening to rush into decisions. What happens if you don't get that job to pay for that car? Uh oh

2. **Refusing to live in the present to create a plan** – Yes, it's nice to think about what could happen, but to get there, you need a list of steps. You need a plan. If you keep fantasizing or thinking about what could happen without a list of steps, all that projection will be is an imagined fantasy. It won't ever be reality. Many of us are dreamers, but don't want to work towards something. Does this describe you?

What's the Positive Alternative to Boost Your Mental Energy?

You need to snap out of projection and fantasy and live in the present. You are not a fortune-teller. You do not have psychic powers, and that's OK.

What you CAN do, however, is positively project into the future, thinking that something will be good, or that it will be worthwhile. When you feel scared, think about the worst-case possibility and logically tell yourself how you might handle it. You can also compare the best- and worst-case scenarios, and see that your fear in the future might be so insignificant compared to the possible best-case scenario, that everything gets dropped and you propel forward (the possible pros far outweigh the cons).

Then, as an adult, you make a list of steps to get you where you need to go. You think about what support systems you have in case something goes wrong. Maybe you can do this quickly in your head to calm yourself, or maybe you need to write it down. The important thing is to proceed forward.

You can't predict the future, but you can think of ways to get to where you need to be, and handle the possible fears you might have. Usually, negative projection stops us from trying when we have the fear of failure, looking silly, rejection, and so on (see the next section for a more thorough discussion on **fear**).

As I said, some fantasy is normal, and can actually be helpful to propel you to work towards a goal. But if you live too much in fantasy or build up stories in your mind (such as sex with someone), you can feel vastly deflated if things don't go your way. This is, again, part of accepting that while this energy is a good propulsion system, you can still never predict what will happen. You snap back to the present and accept what will happen.

Practical Exercises

Select one of the following you think you have issues with:

1. Negative projection

2. Fantasy and positive projection

Negative Projection

You will use a tool: **Negative to Positive Projection**. When you find yourself projecting negatively, instead, flip your thinking into positive projection. Don't ask, "What's the worst thing that can happen?" ask, "What's the best thing that can happen?" and compare the two possibilities. What propels you into the unknown?

Think about IF the worst case were to happen, how you could handle it—because usually, you can handle any situation that arises. I mean, you've survived so far, haven't you? And I'm sure you've been through your fair share of bad stuff!

Talk to a friend about your thoughts on the worst- vs. best-case scenarios. Do they think you are being over-dramatic with your worst case?

In your **journal**, fill in the following table with at least one negative projection occurrence each day, or something that's been troubling you for a while:

Event	Worst Case	Best Case	How Could I Handle the Worst Case?

This will begin to show you the power of positive thinking. If you are going to do a bit of projection, it might as well be positive. Remember: We learned in meditation that we have so many thoughts each day, but usually we cling to those that are negative. Why not cling and give energy to those that are positive? And no matter what, you should be able to handle the worst case if it happens. No matter what!

After considering the positive possibility, get back to the present and get to work on your dream or your goal.

Fantasy and Positive Projection

While a bit of fantasy and positive projection can actually be helpful (see the exercise above), living too much in the future is wasteful, and leads to living the life of a dreamer. If you want something to happen, you need to do the work now. This tool is: **Use It to Manifest Your Dreams!**

With regards to fantasy, you don't KNOW how it will be. You can't. It's more fun to see how it will be in reality. I mean, what's the fun in life if you know exactly what's going to happen? It might decrease anxiety, but it makes things boring.

You can use fantasy and positive projection as a powerful force, though. Usually we fantasize about what we don't have but want. (e.g., about a dreamy guy or girl, a car, going on a trip, and so on). So we're going to stop dreaming, and start taking action. And if you don't want to start taking action, you will drop the fantasy so you can move on to things that deserve your energy.

For three days, notice when you slip into fantasy. Fill out the following table:

Date and Rough Time	What Did I Fantasize About?	My Thoughts and Feelings on This

There should be some themes that keep repeating themselves. Some common ones include:

1. Sex, men/women, dating

2. Traveling/exotic places

3. Luxury items like cars, laptops, new instruments, etc.

4. Having more friends

5. Having more free time

You may have different ones, and that's more than fine.

Decide now - Are these fantasies something you actually want, or could you live without them? Do you need more time for fun? Do you want to be dating other people?

If you can live without them, leave them behind and focus on the present/your life now.

If you want them, it's time to take action to get them. You will need to craft your own goals for each (goal setting is another large topic in and of itself, and I've included a summary in the Extras section). Here's a sample of how you could tackle *having more friends*:

If you want more friends, you need to go to more social events to meet people. This means you might need to cut out activities you currently are doing, but that you do alone. Or, you need to start doing them with others:

- Make a goal of going to one social event every week to start, then later raise it to two or more.

- Search meetup.com for something you are interested in! Is it politics? Video games? Music? Martial arts? There are people out there who like the same things, and chances are you'll find people you have more in common with at these events then somewhere else. Make it easier on yourself, be smart about this!

- Then go. Just go! Tell yourself you will not leave except if you've talked to one person and left with their contact info.

- Give yourself a reward (cookie?) and a round of applause for accomplishing this.

Follow up with that person the next day and arrange to go for coffee or beer...or maybe doing whatever thing you met them at!

In general - You need a logical step-by-step strategy to accomplish your goal and turn the fantasy into reality. No more fantasizing, let's get you LIVING where you want to be. As Henry David Thoreau said:

"Our truest life is when we are in dreams awake."

You can't predict the future, but you can be optimistic about it and know that if anything bad happens, you can handle it.

Fantasy points us towards things we want. If we have most of what we want, fantasy stops. Take action steps to turn your fantasies into reality, or drop them. And accept that you can never completely predict the outcome or how things will be. You need to walk forward, and see what will happen.

Welcome to **exploration**—what you were meant to do both as a child and as an adult.

Another little trick you can use for positive projection is to either create a **vision board** or **place images** of places you want to go or things you would like to achieve everywhere—as your computer and cell phone backgrounds, on your fridge, etc. This burns into your subconscious so you can never let go of it. You know you want to go there, and your mind will not let go until you go, until you take steps towards making these dreams a reality.

My cell phone background for the past few months while writing this book was of buildings in Hong Kong and South East Asia, and I booked my ticket to go in February of 2015 after a few months of those images being constantly around me. Thankfully, I also saved over $1,500 doing it! You can learn more about how to do that yourself here.[1]

Have fun with this. Pictures of places, maybe a nice toy you want...whatever it is, put it where you look most commonly to propel you forward and help you work.

---

[1] See: http://lightwayofthinking.com/how-save-over-1500-book-first-location-independent-move/

Chapter 20.
Fear

"The world is going to explode."
"She's going to make fun of me. I can't."
"What if I look stupid?"
"What if I fail?"

Does this sound familiar? You've always wanted to do something, but you psych yourself out thinking it will be the end of the world if it doesn't go your way. *"What happens if they laugh at me?" "What happens if they don't like me?"*

All this negative energy!

Fear will stop you from living your life. Fear kills dreams.

Why You Might Do It and Where It Comes From

Unfortunately, many of your perceived "problems" in life boil down to what are actually your fears. Some common fears are the:

- Fear of success

- Fear of failure

- Fear of letting go of something that is comfortable (the fear of change)

- Fear of not being good enough

- Fear of something bad happening

- Fear of being imperfect

- Fear of the unknown

- Fear of being judged

Two examples:

Example #1

Many men deal with "approach anxiety," as coined by the men's dating advice groups or pick-up artist community. Simply, this means that they are afraid to go up to a woman that they are interested in and say "Hi." But we've been all been talking for a long time, and saying "Hi" since long before ever thinking about dating. So where does the issue come from?

The "problem" is not the common excuse: "I don't know how to do it or what to say." The guy knows he can.

Is this you? If so:

- You're afraid of being rejected and judged. You think someone's opinion of you has to be your reality, so if they say no to you, then you are worth nothing (how bad is that?!?!)

- You're afraid of not being good enough in their eyes.

- You're afraid of something bad happening (e.g., the woman doesn't like you or want to date you).

- You're afraid of being imperfect (if you say something silly or stumble over your words a bit).

- You're afraid of being uncomfortable (e.g., if there is an awkward silence or you say something weird).

Example #2

I have a problem getting on roller coasters or crazy theme park rides. Actually, I don't really have a problem. I mean, I just buy an entry ticket to an amusement park, wait in line, and get on the ride.

- I'm afraid of the unknown and something bad happening. What if the roller coaster crashes (unlikely given safety checks)? What if I throw up while I'm riding it? That would be embarrassing.

- I'm afraid of being uncomfortable. Again, throwing up. Maybe I can't get off the coaster during the long ride if I don't like it.

- I'm afraid of not being good enough, and being judged. What if the friends I'm with laugh at me if I get scared?

What's the Positive Alternative to Boost Your Mental Energy?

Once you see that most "problems" are actually "fears" (and you can accept that we ALL have fears), and that you're still OK, things get easier.

For example, I know, because of my past, that dating and girls get my fears going, as does meeting new people or any social situation. That comes from being bullied and having women put their needs over mine. Taking risks in general also makes me nervous.

But guess what? You can work on your fears and get over them. **All fears are learned** (except the fear of loud noises and falling, which are primal fears meant to protect us). **If you have learned fears, you can un-learn them**.

You must accept that you have fears, and then move forward anyways. How come some people are cowering in the darkness while others strive forward? The people who feel the fear and do it anyways know that fear is all in the mind, and in the future (which they can't predict, right?). Thus, it is all up to them what they believe. Do they believe they will be OK facing the fear? Do they believe they will survive no matter what, and be happy that they pushed forward?

For me, I didn't want to accept the fear of moving across the world from Canada to Asia, or of starting my own business. I tried to logic my way out of it, but that never works. You can only feel all of your emotions, and then consciously choose how to act.

Finally, it took my friend reminding me to accept my fear (something I have issues with—accepting bad things and emotions) to feel better. I accepted that I'd *feel afraid* no matter what, but can still move forward. I realized I had TONS of support and good things going for me and that I had saved enough money to come back home if I ran into trouble.

And surprisingly, I felt better, even though I still had the fear. I just chose to keep pressing on anyways, putting plans into motion to book my ticket to Asia, and focusing full time on my blog, Light Way of Thinking (http://www.lightwayofthinking.com).

The tools I will give you to deal with fear are not meant to cast fear aside. You'll always have fear, as **nobody is fearless**. The tools are meant to get you going in small bite-size steps to tackle your fears so you can live your life and not always wonder...

"What if?"

Practical Exercises

So there are only two possibilities for fear—accept it and find ways to deal by pushing forward, or be controlled by it.

Not all fears need necessarily be tackled. For example, I fear going to Colombia and getting kidnapped by drug lords, and I don't see a huge need to tackle that fear.

But my fear of dating? I had to and have to get through that—

it's too important to me not to.

Note: As you accomplish items and push through your fears, ensure that you give yourself small **rewards** every step of the way—a new app, a cookie, something that says "*Hey, good job! Keep going!*" It will make you want to do more and more.

- ### Ladder Method for Conquering Fear (Progressive Desensitization)

Refer to the Chapter on **Regret**, which teaches you how to overcome your fears through Cognitive Behavioral Therapy techniques (Chapter 17).

- ### Talking to Others and Penalties

"I'm having issues facing my fear alone. I make up excuses and do nothing, then I feel terrible because I'm not making any progress."

If you are having large issues facing a fear, get a friend to help you, or tell them you will give them money (or face a similar penalty) if you don't take steps towards conquering the fear. Every day, you have to call them to let them know that you did a step on your fear ladder—or you pay them $20.

If you are dreading a big decision—like I did with clicking the button to book my flight ticket from Canada to Asia—call a friend and get them to talk you through it. **It's OK to need help to face your fears, as long as you face them!!**

Letting your fears out and having someone say "It's OK" makes it 1000 times easier to move forward. And also, if you are having trouble, they can support you. Do not be afraid to let people in to help you—you will feel much better for it.

- ### Handling Fears in the Moment - SIHAP

The ladder method is great for planning ahead to have a structured way to face your fears. For example, you can plan to go talk to people if you are afraid—there are set steps and times when you will be socializing.

But what happens if you are somewhere, want to do something then and there, and feel afraid to do it? Are you going to get out a notebook and create a fear ladder? Well I guess you could, but that's kind of impractical...

Sure, if you have consistent problems talking to a friend and accountability is great, but are there ways to push yourself when you want to do something?

Absolutely.

Speed - First, the longer you wait to do something, the greater the sense of anticipation, the more stories your mind builds about what MIGHT happen, the more mental resistance there is, and the more nervous you feel. The faster you do the thing you are afraid of, the better.

Indenting - Think about times when you have done something you have been afraid of. Maybe there is something that is WAY scarier than what you are thinking of doing right now. For example, I've traveled across Europe for two months by myself, getting lost, dealing with stressful situations, and making friends along the way. Comparing that to saying "Hi" to someone at a social event in my home town, I can say, *"Well what I did before was WAY harder and had A LOT more risk involved, and I survived. I'm sure I can handle this and it will be OK."* Indenting is a process of comparison.

Have I Accomplished This Before? - If you have done a similar thing before (i.e., you have pushed through the fear already), then logically you should be able to do it again! Once you do it, you can always do it—as long as you are still you—even if you FEEL more scared.

Affirmations - Tell yourself *"I can handle it," "I'll be OK,"* and "*I can always call a friend if something goes bad.*"

Projection - Think about what you could gain from doing this thing. Think about how it could go well, and how good you will feel after. If it's traveling somewhere new, then what will you see and experience? If it's talking to someone, what type of connection could you make? Always, always, always assume the positive.

Try each of these methods and see if they help you. As with all of the tools, do not try to do everything all at once. Build up the positive habits slowly, trying one for one week, then another the next week, and so on.

You aren't scared of being bad, you're frustrated because you think you could be doing so much more, and something is holding you back. Start fighting! Be OK with fear, accept that it's normal and that EVERYONE—the old man in the rocking chair, the runway model, and me—has fears. The difference between the strong and the weak is that there are those who are courageous and brave enough to fight against their fears, versus those that give up and shrink in the face of them.

Are you willing to be strong?

"Our deepest fear is not that we are inadequate. Our deepest fear is that we are powerful beyond measure." - Marianne Williamson

Chapter 21.
Anxiety and Worry

"I'm not going to get there on time!"
"What if the world implodes?"
"What if there's too much salt?!"
"AHHHHHHHHHHHHHHHHHHHHHHHH."

Anxiety is something quite personal to me because I've struggled with it a great deal, and still do. You feel like things will come down with specific activities, or the world's going to end in general. The feeling is usually associated with chest tightness, shortness of breath, and just feeling uneasy.

The unfortunate thing about anxiety is that it is quite personal. There are umbrella terms like *generalized anxiety disorder* or *social anxiety*, but everyone feels anxiety slightly differently and under different circumstances.

Why You Might Do It and Where It Comes From

Anxiety and fear are interrelated. For example:

1. **The fear of the unknown/what you don't have control over/something bad happening** - Because your mind fears what it doesn't know or what will happen, it makes you feel nervous or scared. This can most likely be due to negative projection (see **Projection**, Chapter 19) and assuming the worst thing will happen, when in actuality you have no idea.

2.   **The fear of failure** - Your anxiety says you might try something but you'll suck at it, it won't work, or it won't be good enough. Due to expecting perfection or things to go completely smooth, you get those nervous tinges that prevent you from moving forward.

Any of the fears discussed in Chapter 20 can be tied closely to anxiety.

Those who suffer from anxiety usually have been through traumatic experiences as children that made them think that the world was unsafe. The world turned from a place of exploration and adventure to one where things much be checked constantly in case something goes wrong. In effect, having them NOT be children. Such experiences could be:

•   Harsh criticism from parents or other authority figures

•   Abuse situations

•   Bullying and social ostracization

You learned that things were scary, so your brain and body must be in constant flight-or-fight mode, and you usually choose flight versus fight due to the uncomfortable feelings. You learned about the amygdala in the introduction section in Chapter 5 and how it is responsible for many stored memories and emotions. Those who have an overactive amygdala are constantly in a state of anxiety.

Trust me: I know it sucks. I used to walk around as a neurotic ball of anxious energy. I'm far from perfect these days, but man has my anxiety gone down, and I never want to go back to the way I was.

The **anxiety** leads to worry…about what might happen. Anxiety is an emotion we cannot control, but **worrying** will not do anything except burn your brain up.

What's the Positive Alternative to Boost Your Mental Energy?

Deeper issues that lead to anxiety require therapy to be solved. However, we can take positive steps to help alleviate the anxiety.

Instead of worrying, we're going to use a series of practical exercises to get you to take action.

Practical Exercises

1. **Focus on your meditation** - Not only should you be doing 30 minutes a day regularly (or more), but you can also meditate while you are walking, eating, etc. You are RIGHT there. Anxiety comes from living in the mind and the future, and making yourself be where you are every moment throughout the day will really help you. If you aren't predicting the future and are OK in the present all the time, you must be fine.

2. **Facing your fears** - Again, anxiety stems from fear. Tackling your fears and SHOWING yourself that things will be OK is the only way to re-program your brain. You need proof. To do this, you step your way slowly up to what you want to do. The cognitive behavioral therapy exercise with **regret** (Chapter 17) will help you get here. You can also read the section on **fear** (Chapter 20).

3. **Talking to others** - If there is something you feel INCREDIBLY anxious about, talk to a trusted friend, counselor, or therapist...someone whom you know will understand. **EVERYONE** has anxiety and fears, but people handle them differently. The point is to see that everyone gets scared sometimes, but usually the fears aren't so bad. I already talked about some of my fears in the **Fear** section, but to reiterate: Talking to girls makes me nervous, as do social situations. Not doing things perfectly makes me anxious and

78

sometimes stops me from doing them at all. I get frustrated and nervous when I can't do everything that I want to get done in one day. Trust me, everyone gets anxious, but letting it out will help. And also, if and when you tackle your fears, talk to someone about your triumphs and struggles! Having support there will be REALLY helpful.

4. **Positive and supportive self-talk** - Many times, anxiety gets to us because we believe the thoughts in our mind that say *"Things are dangerous,"* and *"AHHHHH, RUN LIKE YOUR ASS IS ON FIRE!"* Try talking to yourself as you would a close friend who is scared about something. Would you tell them *"Yeah, you SHOULD be scared. You're going to die!"* Probably not. You might understand that whatever they worry about is scary, but that if they did it, they'd be OK...aside from possibly swimming with alligators. I don't recommend that. For a more detailed outline of positive self-talk, see Chapter 29. There, I include a LONG list of possible affirmations to help make you feel better and stronger.

5. **Five Minutes of Space** - Most of the time in life we are rushing so much and being so hard on ourselves for not doing more, moving faster, or performing up to some standard. Even when we feel bad, tired, or burned out, something says, *"Keep going, or else you suck."* Five Minutes of Space is designed to protect against this. You probably spend more than five minutes a day on your cell phone, e-mail, Facebook, etc.... So, either at a specific time or when you feel REALLY stressed, **STOP**. Sit or stand wherever you are and just be, meditating with eyes open or eyes closed. Listen to what is around you, feel the ground beneath you, and feel your breath going in and out. Realize that any thoughts you have of not doing enough, things coming crashing down, etc., all stem from your mind, but here and now in this moment you are OK. It's pretty peaceful here, isn't it? After doing this, I assure you that you will feel refreshed and less stressed. However, for someone who is used to operating at 110% breakneck speed the entire day, this can be challenging, so start with one minute first and

work your way up to five.

6.   **20-Minute Buffer** - Many anxious people worry about the subway messing up, them needing extra time because they forget to pack a lunch, and so on. Instead of trying to change your anxious nature, you need to work with it and accept that it's going to be an issue, so you need to put things into place to handle it. Adding 20-minute buffers (spaces before and after) to your appointments can really help curb your anxiety, because if something messes up, you'll still be on time. Whenever you set an appointment, such as for work, a date, and so on, plan to be ready for 20 minutes before. This simple step will save you lots of stress and also stops you from jamming too much into one day.

7.   **Move Slower** - Anxious people are great at being whirling dervishes—moving from A to B to C at light speed. The problem is that while they are busy moving so fast, life slips right by and they have no time to enjoy it. They are also afraid that they can't stop or things will come crashing down. By making a decision to consciously move slower and not rush through everything, your quality of work and life will increase. Is it better to do more (**quantity**), or enjoy more and do things better (**quality**)? I think you know the answer. If you are used to moving INCREDIBLY fast, move at half your usual speed and see what happens.

Journaling and Accountability

The more of the exercises you implement, the more tools you have to deal with your anxiety. But you should focus on one or two at a time, so your attention isn't spread too thin.

Follow this table for an outline of journaling and accountability depending upon which exercises you have selected:

Exercise	What to Journal/ For Accountability
1. Meditation	1. How long did you meditate each day? 2. Are you reaching your goals/consecutively increasing the time? 3. How do you feel afterwards?
2. Facing Your Fears	1. What fear are you currently tackling? 2. What are your steps to build up to tackling the larger fear (see **regret**, Chapter 20, for detailed information). What happened when you faced your fear, are you still alive (hint: if you're writing, obviously everything went OK). 3. How did you feel after you faced the fear, or moved a step closer to facing the fear? Are you motivated to keep going?

3. Talking to Others	1. What did you choose to talk about and why?
	2. Whom did you talk to?
	3. What did they say? Did they say you were silly? Did they understand?
	4. How do you feel after talking to someone? Relieved? Better prepared to face fear? Deflated? A bit embarrassed? Why?
4. Positive and Supportive Self-Talk	1. What are some things you can tell yourself to feel better?
	2. What did you say and how did you feel afterwards?
	3. To really see the power of positive self-talk, try being hard, critical, and mean to yourself in another situation. Notice the difference in how you feel afterwards and your motivation. Write down how you feel. What do you think this shows you? What conclusions can you draw?

5. Five Minutes of Space	1. What time did you decide to do this (if you set a time)? 2. Were you able to do it today? Why or why not? 3. How did you feel BEFORE doing it? 4. How did you feel AFTER doing it?
6. 20 Minute Buffer	1. What appointments have you added the buffer for? 2. How does it feel having the extra time to prepare for things? Do you feel more or less stressed?
7. Move Slower	1. What kind of thoughts did you hear as you moved slower? 2. Do you think they became true? 3. How did you feel moving slower? More relaxed? More stressed? 4. Did things come crashing down because you did less?

For a long time I wished my anxiety away. I only started really succeeding more in life when I realized and accepted that I have an anxious personality type, and I can't fight that. I can find ways to help myself through things with planning, learning to say no, getting proper sleep, and so on...but I cannot fight anxiety.

Once you accept that you might have anxiety in a few situations but realize you can **STILL MOVE FORWARD DESPITE THE ANXIETY, AND THAT ANXIETY IS NORMAL,** life gets a whole lot better.

This assumes that your anxiety is not detrimental to the point where you are afraid to leave the house. If your anxiety is at this level, you may need to seek professional counselling and possibly medication in the short term so you can instill new habits into your mind that enable you to function well in day-to-day life. (**Note**: I endorse use of medication in the short term if prescribed by a certified professional so that you can learn new habits. I do not endorse living on medication for the rest of your life. Medication and therapy should be pursued at the same time.)

The fight against anxiety is life-long, but once you stop viewing it as a "fight" and work towards accepting it by learning ways to deal with it, that is when you can truly start living.

Section VI

Mental Wastes of the Present

Chapter 22.
Complaining

"It's not fair that I don't get weekends off."
"I can't believe the line at this place!"

So many of us waste huge amounts of energy **complaining**. You aren't happy with your situation, so you vent your frustration. *"Why me?" "Why can't I change?"* Blah blah blah.

Sorry, that may sound harsh, but now that I've changed from being a complainer to someone who takes action, I can't stand complaining. If I sense myself doing it, I try to silence it right away because I know how bad it is for my well-being—and I need you to know that too.

Why You Might Do It and Where It Comes From

The act of complaining stems from one of three things:

1.   Refusing to accept the present or wanting everything to go your way.

2.   Not knowing how to change something you'd like to change and becoming frustrated.

3.   Fear of changing something you want to change.

Most of the time, once you really think about what you are doing when you are complaining, it seems silly. Usually the answer is simple. Or, it comes down to a **fear**.

Example #1

"*I'm sad I'm single.*"

"So why don't you go meet people?"

"*I don't know how.*"

"What do you mean? Just go to some social events and talk to people, and if you find someone who is cute, just tell them that and ask for their number."

"*No way, that's too scary.*"

Example #2

"*I couldn't believe how long the line was at the post office today.*"

"What time did you go?"

"*After work.*"

"Man, that's when everybody goes! Why didn't you go when it opens? That way NOBODY would be there! Nobody wants to get up early, haha!"

"*F*** that, I'm not getting up early. It should be good when I go.*"

Example #3

"*I can't believe my boss made me work on the weekend again, I hate my job.*"

"So why don't you quit or find something else?"

"*No way, the pay is too good and I like the benefits.*"

"Why don't you find a better job with similar benefits and pay?"

"Too lazy, that's too much work and I don't have the time."

"Uhhh..."

I think you see the point.

What's the Positive Alternative To Boost Your Mental Energy?

Take any situation you are complaining about. You have two options:

1. If the situation is out of your control, accept it, and learn for the future (e.g., you know NEVER to go to the post office after work again).

2. If you can do something about your situation (like you being unhappy with your job), DO SOMETHING. Stop wasting energy complaining and move forward, taking action.

Practical Exercises

Maybe you complain so much and are so used to not taking action that you need de-programming. If you want to make a big change in your cognitive processes, I recommend the **No Complaint Experiment**, or **NCE**.

Timothy Ferriss discussed how Will Bowen, a Kansas City minister, designed an experiment to get his congregation to stop complaining.[1] Ferriss altered Bowen's original exercise a bit, and that's the one I will present here:

Place a band of some sort around one of your wrists. Every time you complain, you move the band from one side of your body to the other wrist. For 21 days, the challenge is to never move the band. If you move it, the countdown starts again.

A "complaint" for our purposes will be complaining with no action for the present or the future.

So *"I hate my job and it sucks"* is a complaint.

But *"I hate my job, and it sucks, so I'm going to start looking for new ones"* is not...as long as you ACTUALLY TAKE STEPS TO GET THAT NEW JOB! For example, you tailor your C.V. one day, look online for jobs another, etc.

Journaling and Accountability

While doing the NCE, or if you simply notice that there's an area you keep complaining about, write down what it is. Now what are the action steps you can take to move forward on it?

No, it's not sexy, but it's logical and gets you out of victim mode. The point is to move forward and do something instead of being mired in negative emotions. Those negative emotions are telling you to DO something so you can be happier. LISTEN TO THEM.

Hate your job? Find a new one. Where can you look for new ones? Find websites or job boards. Make days when you will do job applications. Make a day when you will edit your C.V. Plan it out.

Tired of being single? Where can you find cool people? Commit to going to one social event a week and getting three numbers from single people.

For all anxiety or victim mentality issues, action is always the answer.

Complaining comes from a childlike state of being helpless, unable to do anything. Usually, it's because you were feeling afraid, powerless, or un-sure of what to do. Don't let that carry over into adulthood. You are now grown up and it's up to you to go grab what you want. If you can't do it yourself, find people who can help you.

The world waits for no one, so get livin'!

---

[1] Ferriss, Timothy. *Real Mind Control: The 21-Day No-Complaint Experiment*. The Blog Of Tim Ferriss: Experiments in Lifestyle Design. Retrieved from http://fourhourworkweek.com/2007/09/18/real-mind-control-the-21-day-no-complaint-experiment on January 7th, 2015.

Chapter 23.
Excuses

"I can't."
"It's too hard."
"I'm tired."

Why You Might Do It and Where It Comes From

Excuses usually originate from one of two feelings:

1. You feel too scared to do something.

2. You feel lazy, and it's easier to do something else instead.

One of the most common excuses is that of not having enough time. I mean, with such a busy schedule, how can you do everything you need to?

You find time and MAKE time for what is important to you. Period.

If you aren't making time, it's because you really don't want to do something, or it's too hard, or maybe it's not a priority right now. You don't want to give up something you find easy or comfortable (for example, watching TV) for something that seems to involve a lot of effort (going to the gym). Excuses sound best to the person who is making them, but they are usually just brain farts.

What's the Positive Alternative To Boost Your Mental Energy?

Taking action. Simple.

Practical Exercise

When you hear yourself making excuses, think about this:

1. What am I making an excuse about?

2. Am I avoiding this because it is hard, I might fail, or I feel scared?

3. How important is this thing to me?

Based on the answers to these questions, you must either move forward and DO something, or drop whatever you are making an excuse about. Just like **complaining**, excuses are a symptom of not wanting to get past some type of inertia, or giving up a comfortable activity in favor of one that could serve you better.

Journaling and Accountability

If you decide an activity is not important enough, then it can be dropped. It may be good to check in with a trusted friend to see if what you are dropping really isn't that important. For example: I once had a period in my life where I wanted to drop dating, but it wasn't because I didn't care at the time—it was because I felt too afraid to actually work up the nerve to talk to people. After getting over a lot of social anxiety, I can usually figure out when I'm more feeling nervous about talking to women vs. when it's not on my priority list and I'd prefer to be doing something else.

If you decide that an activity IS important and needs to be done, then take at least a tiny small step towards getting it done. Set small benchmarks and steps to achieve a certain goal and GO HIT

THEM! For dating, it might be saying hi to someone every day and going to one social event per week. For a physical injury, it might be stretching every day. For not having enough time alone, it might be marking a 30-minute period each day where NOTHING is allowed to get in your way.

Whatever it is, do SOMETHING. DOING SOMETHING IS BETTER THAN DOING NOTHING.

Excuses are useless wastes of energy. Move forward with your life, you've only got one! Decide to either handle something (if it's important and if you can), or drop it completely. Excuses make life miserable, while taking action makes life fun! Handle one excuse at a time and continually improve upon life.

Chapter 24.
Churning and Spiraling

"I might fail if I go overseas to find a job. What if I starve? How am I going to survive? What will I do? What if I can't find friends? Maybe I should look into possible options for jobs. But I want to take a specific job! I don't like working at other places. I wanna live my dream! What if I fail at my dream though, will people laugh at me?"

Ahhhhhhhhhhhh, too many words, it's hurting my brain! As of writing this book, the above thought is actually something I was churning on. I got my Master's degree in engineering, traveled Europe for three months, and then decided to open up a freelance writing firm. After two months I realized I wasn't having fun, and then I was faced with the choice of possibly pursuing my blog and book writing/course creation full time.

The problem is that I had to use my savings, and if I ran out of money I might look like an idiot, and then what would I do?

Why You Might Do It and Where It Comes From

Churning or spiraling come from the tendency to live in the mind, which is why it is ESSENTIAL to learn how to meditate, be present, and get out of the mind as quickly as possible. All living in the mind makes you want to do is live there more and...well, you see where it gets you.

Churning is like trying to get out of quicksand: The more you listen to a thought, the more it drags you in, and the more you feel like

95

you can't shake it. While this is obviously not desirable for bad thoughts like *"I'm going to fail,"* it can be hurtful to you for positive thoughts as well. You may live too much in the mind versus being in the real world. Of course it's preferable to churn on a good thought, but churning just creates tension.

Another compounding issue is churning and **confirmation bias**. Confirmation bias is a psychological term that refers to how you may search for evidence to support a decision based on a pre-disposed emotion. When applied to how you feel about yourself—say if you have low self-esteem—you may look for evidence to support the fact that you are a worm, even when you are really an amazing person. You completely ignore all your good qualities and focus on the negative. You also interpret everything to support the fact that you are, indeed, a worm.

This is a huge cornerstone in the cause of depressive thinking and thoughts.

So the fact that a girl does not text you back is proof that you are not worthy of love and attention, and then you churn on being worthless, how you always fail with women, how you are a loser, and so on. Or...maybe she saved you from wasting your time chasing her.

The fact that someone didn't smile at you means they don't like you, you can't make people happy, you need to rely on other people's validation, and can't be happy yourself. Or, maybe they are having a bad day and you might need to cheer them up!

You can read more about the confirmation bias, and how it works with anxiety and depression here.[1]

What's the Positive Alternative To Boost Your Mental Energy?

First, it's living in the present, and trying to stay out of the mind.

Woohoo, that was easy, but amidst a meditation practice sometimes it's hard to do that. Sometimes it's hard to let go of a thought.

Practical Exercises

Usually you churn because something that's important is not getting taken care of. So, if you feel scared about something, you probably need to air out the emotions. If you can't shake a thought or two that keep coming up, they may be pointing to something that you want handled. But that might involve work, a chance of failure, or risk. For example, preparing for a trip, dating more people, or finding out how to have more free time.

Other churning possibilities could be related to anxiety and depression, such as churning initiation thoughts like *"I suck," "I'm bad,"* or *"I'm not good enough and nobody loves me."*

You'll have to be the judge of this.

The best way I've found to deal with this is by talking to a trusted friend and getting their input on the situation. Usually, if you are trapped in your mind, you need someone who is external to your thought patterns—they can usually set you straight. This might help show you that what you are worrying about is a) normal, or b) not as big of a deal as you think. Either way, this helps gets you into a better state of mind so that you can either lean in to what you are afraid of, or set steps to tackle the specific fear (see **fear**, Chapter 20).

If you are stuck in a negative thought pattern, such as *"I'm bad,"* a friend can also help show you that, hey, you might not be perfect, you might have bad days, but that's OK. You are still an amazing person and don't need to beat yourself up. Beating yourself up is just counter-productive, and being negative only hurts you!

Some other suggestions:

- ## **Problems in the Moment—Do It Now or Drop It**

Sometimes you churn over an action you would like to take RIGHT now, and go back and forth saying *"Yes I'll do it"* and *"No, it does not matter, it's not necessary."* The easiest example I can think of, coming from personal experience, was when I was trying to improve my dating skills: When I saw a woman I wanted to talk to walking around, on the subway, or somewhere public, I would have many thoughts telling me I should go say hi, but others saying that I'm putting too much pressure on myself, it's not necessary, and I can meet someone later.

I have found and accepted that, personally, this will always be a struggle for me. But, I prefer to spend my time walking around reading, listening to music, or meditating instead of worrying about my sex and dating life. I also know that if I am in a public place and someone really catches my attention, that I will go up to them. And I make sure to go to social events to meet people. The thoughts will always be there, but how much attention do I need to pay to them? Do I really want to ruin my peaceful core?

- ## **Problems in the Present Moment—Will This Matter in X Time?**

Another thing I love to ask myself when I am worrying about something is:

"Will this matter in two hours?"

"Two days?"

"Two weeks?"

"Two months?"

"Two years?"

"When I am old and frail?"

We make big deals about things that are usually quite

inconsequential when it comes to our entire lives, stressing ourselves out for no reason. I'm very good at this and need constant reminders to relax.

Things seem to be so important in the present, and we experience strong emotional reactions. But over the long haul, they won't matter at all.

Guy didn't text you back? You probably won't even care in a year when you meet other people (if you keep going out).

Didn't get that job? Probably won't matter in two years after you find a new one that you love (if you keep applying and searching).

I remember when I was a teenager, stressing for two hours between two different ski jackets that were both of comparable price, just a bit of a different look. If I had known to ask myself the "Will this matter" question, do you know how much time and stress I would have saved myself? It's just a stupid ski jacket! Oh well, we learn as we grow!

The next time you are having issues, try asking yourself that question and see what happens. You might find that some things are just too silly to even think about.

- **Re-direction**

Many people try to control negative thoughts. While you can aim to replace negative thoughts with good ones through the use of passive tools, give negative thoughts less energy, and so on, you can't get rid of them. Those that are quite positive are just incredibly adept at dismissing negative thoughts and not believing their minds.

So if you can't control them, how do you get out of a situation where it feels like you are spiraling or churning into a constant negative thought stream?

The answer is to quickly re-focus your attention to something else. If you can, quickly direct your attention to your breathing, your feet touching the ground, or any other sensation on your body that brings you out of the mind. Otherwise, do a different activity: Go run around the block, wash some dishes, talk to someone...anything that re-directs your attention and cuts the negative thoughts before they start.

If you believe you have issues with a lot of spiraling into negative thoughts, it is worth journaling down at least once a day the details of a spiral:

• When did this start? What event caused it?

• What time did this happen?

• Has this happened before (similar event or time)?

• How did you get out of the spiral, or attempt to get out of it?

• You may start to notice certain patterns, like you are more negative in the morning, or a specific person causes you grief. But, you will be able to jump out of the thoughts and not believe them. Or, you can begin to make changes to keep these spirals from occurring.

• **Write It Out**

If you are churning on a certain thought or situation, take out your journal or any blank piece of paper and write. Put the thought or item at the top of the page and write until you can't write anymore. Set a timer for at least five minutes and go.

Usually, churning relates to stuck thoughts and emotions, and you must release as you would vent a steam valve. You can release them through verbal expression (with a friend), or via writing on paper. These may serve as venting vessels, and you will no longer need to do anything further; or it may show you what is going on inside your head.

The key here with either verbal or written expression is to NOT FILTER yourself. Sometimes, if the thought is more personal, it might be better to stick to written expression (at least at first) so you can write without fear of any external judgment. Then, if you feel safe, you can open up to someone else.

I have found that churning is a symptom of living in the mind, and a prime cause of anxiety. As you become better able to handle anxiety in general, enjoy life more, or get out of your head (e.g., through exercise, laughing with friends, etc.), your tendency to churn will go down.

Churning can also be a symptom of trying to control every possible outcome. Unfortunately, we cannot control the future. We can take certain precautions and prepare for the future, but then we must just dive forward and see what happens. It might be scary, but such is part of the adventure of life. If we treat life as an adventure, things become far more fun and enjoyable...even in the down times.

I'm not saying that what you are churning about isn't difficult, tough, scary, depressing, or undeserving of your mental energy. Even thoughts such as *"I'm bad"* need your mental energy so you can understand where they are coming from and work to lessen them.

What I am saying is that churning usually goes far into the realm of unnecessary thinking, and can be hurtful. *"Put some thought into this,"* as an undergrad professor of mine used to say, but then take action and live in life to see what happens.

Don't over think.

...It gives you wrinkles.

---

[1] See: http://lightwayofthinking.com/confirmation-bias-emotions-screwing-over/

Chapter 25.
Trying to Remember Everything

"I have to wash the dog, go to work, do the spreadsheet, talk to Doug, and do my goals for the year. Oh right! For those goals I was thinking of setting benchmarks X, Y, and Z..."

I'm already exhausted.

Most people have amazing ideas and a CRAPLOAD of stuff to do during the day.

Yet they believe that they can remember it all, and won't forget anything.

You are awesome, for sure—but you are only human. Ever had that fleeting thought, and then you try to recall it with a friend, even in a conversation where a minute passes, and then...

Oh crapshoot, it's gone...and you don't know if it's going to come back, ever.

In this case, it's not super important to know where it comes from. It's more important to know the positive alternative.

What's the Positive Alternative to Boost Your Mental Energy?

WRITE IT DOWN.

Everything.

Use notebooks, software, whatever works for you (I'll give you the tools that really help me in a bit). Why force yourself to remember things when you have tools and options for letting SOMETHING ELSE DO IT FOR YOU!

Your job is to come up with the ideas and procedures of how to execute in life. Let something else remember how you want those ideas to be done! This is also a staple in being productive—free up your mental energy any way you can, so you can focus on what you need to do during the day.

Practical Exercises

- ### Use a Calendar

Instead of trying to track all of your appointments, commitments, and what you have to fit in during the day, use a calendar app to do so in advance. That way, you have far less mental strain when deciding what you can and cannot do during the day. I personally use Google Calendar because I'm an Android geek and everything is synched with my Google account, but you could easily use another application or the Mac variant. Whatever works for you.

- ### Keep Notebooks

Keep a notebook beside your bed and a smaller one on your person/in your bag/in your jacket. Anytime you think of something and don't want to forget it, just jot it down. You can always recall it or file it later. The notebook beside the bed can be especially useful if some brilliant idea comes to you while nodding off, but you don't want to pursue it right then. This also keeps your mind from running as you sleep. You definitely want to make sure that thought doesn't disappear into thin air...only to be done by someone else in three months (it's happened).

- ### Use Evernote

Evernote is a program that simulates notebooks. You can

create various notebooks and have as many notes inside them as you want. I find Evernote very useful for keeping track of random ideas that continue on, like a note I have that is a brain dump of all my blog post ideas.

- **<u>Text Yourself</u>**

A quick way to get a reminder!

Less stuff up in your head, more freedom to act, think, and move now...and less stress too.

Chapter 26.
Jealousy and Envy

*"Why can't I have that? Why do they get it and I don't? I wish I was
there to get it too!"*
"I have nothing, I want what they have."

We all know these two cousins. Someone tells us about something
they have or did, and we want it. We see people with certain things
and we say we want them too. Then we get all distraught craving
things we don't have, forgetting about all we do have or have done.

Driving ourselves into even more insanity, even if we want
something and get it...we hear about something else that we don't
have, and start wanting that thing. It's an endless madness!

There have been many times where I used to want a certain
experience so bad and then got it, such as international travel for the
first time. But then I craved more of the same again and again, and
when I heard other people having similar experiences I'd say, *"Oh,
why wasn't I there!? I wish I was! Why can't it be different!?"*

Why You Might Do It and Where It Comes From

Comparison to other people never gets you anywhere (see
Chapter 34 for a more detailed discussion). In short, it is unfair to
compare yourself to other people because they have different moods,
ways of working, and connections. You have things they'll never have
too! As the saying goes, while you were busy wishing you were
someone else or had their talents, someone else was concurrently

wishing they were you.

Many times, jealousy and envy come from external factors—someone has a significant other and you wish YOU had one too. Someone had an experience and YOU wish you had it as well. The problem is that relying on external validation to make you happy is like relying on drugs to make you feel good: They will wear off eventually, no matter what you do. The more you make yourself less affected and reliant on external validation, the better.

In childhood, you learned somewhere that you were never good enough, or needed to constantly compare yourself to others to ensure that you were OK. You did not seek approval from yourself, but rather from others (such as in the case of being bullied or with overly critical parents), and this has transferred into your adult life.

As humans, we'll always want more of what we don't have. Or, more accurately, our minds will always want more of what we don't have. It's an endless stream of "keeping up with the Joneses," and can never end, trying to fill some gaping hole in our lives, thinking that after the next experience (or if we get it) we'll be happy and satiated. You might refer to this as status anxiety, because we are getting anxious over having more of something.

Unfortunately, the truth is that you'll never be satisfied after getting more. No matter what you get, you'll always want something more, because you'll realize that you CAN always have more.

Sucks, eh?

So what can you do?

What's the Positive Alternative to Boost Your Mental Energy?

Pushing down feelings of jealousy is a VERY bad thing to do—that will make them worse.

First, draw yourself back into the present. Usually, feelings of jealousy and envy come from imagining what would happen if YOU were there, or if you were someone else. But that's not your reality right now (fortunately or unfortunately).

The way I think is:

1. Stop. Think about what's going on. You're comparing yourself to other people, but you aren't them. That's madness! You'll never be them!

2. No external thing is going to make me happy. It will give me a temporary rush for sure, but I know it won't make me happy forever. I've seen that multiple times (realize that when you've gotten something like a partner, raise, etc., you didn't stay at super elevated states forever).

3. What one person has or has done, another can get or do. Which means that if I want that experience, I can have it! Maybe it wouldn't be EXACTLY the same, but I could do it (find a girlfriend, go travel, start a business, etc.). In fact, it will be more special because it would be my own unique variant!

4. If I still have time in life, there's no reason why I can't have that thing if I put myself out there!

5. If I really want that thing, that means I need to be planning steps to try and achieve it.

It may seem overly logical, but again, that's what you're trying to do. You feel every emotion sent your way because you can't push them down, but then you use your logical brain to talk to your emotional brain about what's going on.

At times, the jealousy or envy comes out of spite when someone has something you think you DESERVE or should have. This is because you know you can get it but are scared of going out to do it. You'll have to look inside yourself to see what's really going on.

The final step is being **GRATEFUL** for what you already have and have done.

So often, we get caught up in feelings of jealousy or envy and we forget about all we have or have done. Again, we get caught up in the rat race of having more and more items or experiences, and cast aside everything we've already gotten.

This can either be done the moment jealous feelings come up, and you can remember another time when you wanted something else, you got jealous, but then you eventually got that thing. You realize that these feelings are irrational and will always come. You can never win, since there's always more to get! You might as well be happy for all you have, or go find those experiences yourself, enjoying the journey as you progress.

You can also do this every day at a set time to make you realize how fortunate you are for what you have right now, or what you have experienced. I find that, a lot of the time, that makes the feelings of jealousy disappear, or far easier to handle.

Practical Exercises

- **Gratitude Exercise and Practice**

Set aside 10 minutes each morning or night to write in a gratitude journal. I find that HAND writing it is much better than on a computer, but you can experiment with what works for you. Write five things you are grateful for today. You don't have to stretch too hard. It could be that you have food, internet access, the ability to read, good friends and family. This exercise will make you realize all you have instead of constantly wanting something else, which is an endless portal to hell.

- **Why Am I Jealous and What Am I Going to Do About It?**

Pick one time when you felt jealous today and answer the

following in your journal:

1. What did I get jealous about?

2. Has this happened before? Does it keep happening?

3. Do I actually want this—is it something I've desired for a long time? Or is it something I really don't need?

4. If I don't want it, I should let it pass. If I do, I will create action steps I can take to get it. (For example, if it's a girlfriend, you must go out at least one night a week to a social event. If it's a trip, you need to put aside 10% of your paycheck every month. And so on.)

5. Tell a trusted person about your quest if you are moving forward and get feedback on your action steps.

Jealousy can either beat you down, or you can use it as a tool to show you what you'd like to have in your life. Either way, don't waste time on the thoughts. Either drop them, or go get what you want.

Chapter 27.
Perfectionism

"It's not good enough yet."

The problem is that it will NEVER be good enough.

Something inside you says you CAN'T try X, you CAN'T do X. You need to plan more, there can't be ANY hiccups or mistakes, and you need it to be absolutely perfect.

And so you **procrastinate**, continuously putting things off. You tell yourself you don't feel like doing something right now, or that you need to feel a bit better before doing it. THEN it will finally be ready. THEN you will finally be prepared.

I think you know that all of this is a huge problem and a lie to yourself.

Why You Might Do It and Where It Comes From

At the heart of perfectionism are two fears: the fear of judgment (criticism for low quality work and you then being a bad person) and the fear of failure (releasing or doing something and it going bad).

Sometime in your past you learned that if you screwed up A BIT, then there would be serious consequences. Or, you had parents who never expressed appreciation for you just as you were, and always kept pushing you forward. "That's great, but you can do better."

Yes, it's human nature to always strive to be better. But without proper appreciation for all that you are and have done, you create an extremely screwed up cycle of constantly competing with yourself, trying to reach a higher, unattainable, perfect version of you...the perfect version where you get EVERYTHING done in a day (yet you could always do more, couldn't you?), have amazing friends (but they could ALWAYS be better, right?), start dating a beautiful significant other (but they have some annoying quirks), etc. The perfectionism spreads to the people around you too, and you silently judge them.

Oy.

I grew up with a critical and perfectionistic father. In one way this helped me, because I now always strive to be better and put out outstanding, quality work. In another way it hurt me because nothing, even me, seems to ever be good enough. This led to a great deal of sadness, depression, and not realizing all the talents I had even as I continued to improve.

I remember one time I brought home a test in high school, saying,

"Hey Dad, check it out! I got perfect!"

"How did everybody else do?"

"Ummm...I think a lot of people did well, some did OK."

"Hmm...doesn't sound like it was that hard of a test to me."

No worries here. While I still have some issues with my dad (as we all do), I love the snot out of the guy and have some very fond memories of him.

What's the Positive Alternative to Boost Your Mental Energy?

Perfectionism can be a force for good, fueling you to be better. But, it can also make you throw away the gifts you have right now, and create a voice in your head that says, *"You aren't ready."*

You need to read more books on conversation—you aren't ready to talk to people.

You need to edit your writing more—you aren't ready to release it.

You need to figure out what sport would be the best use of your time—better to do more research.

As you can see, sometimes perfectionism is illogical and hilarious.

Being grateful for all you have done and are right now—and setting deadlines—can help fight perfectionism. So can knowing that it's OK to make a mistake, and that nobody is 100% "ON" all the time.

Every time I release an article, I'm worried that it won't be OK. But people usually like it, and I can always edit it later. There's something about making a decision that makes perfectionists scared, because now something is FINAL. Now something has been RELEASED. Now it can be JUDGED. But the alternative—sitting, stagnating, and getting nothing done—is not living life. This also creates a lot of stress because the amount of things to do will keep piling up.

But what about when perfectionism infects our judgment of others? We expect ourselves to be perfect, and that spreads to needing others to always be on time, never lazy, articulate, read good books, not slack off, etc. In a sort of law of transference, the degree to which you expect yourself to be perfect will be the degree to which you expect others to be perfect—you will treat others as you treat yourself.

You need to work on loosening your expectations and being

kinder to yourself and those around you.

Practical Exercises

- ### <u>Being Grateful</u>

See the gratitude exercise in Chapter 26, which talks about **jealousy and envy**.

- ### <u>Positive Self-Talk About Yourself and Others</u>

Self-talk (Chapter 29) gets its own section in this book because it affects a HUGE portion of your life. It is important to know that telling yourself you can always work harder, you suck, you're lazy, etc., does no good for you. All it does is beat you down and make you feel terrible.

One of the fundamental techniques in cognitive behavioral therapy for fighting anxiety and depression is increasing positive self-talk, and here you will focus specifically on what you do.

You could always "do better," but that doesn't mean you haven't done something amazing. This is different for every person, but it usually involves your output to the world (such as the work you do and the conversations you have).

Whenever you hear yourself being critical and perfectionistic, try saying the following thoughts instead:

"I did a good job, and I can always do better. But I'm learning and that's awesome!"

"There's always tomorrow to do work, but I did a lot today."

"I guess I could have done X better, but it still turned out pretty great. Nothing's perfect!"

"Hey, it's better than not doing anything at all! At least I gave it a shot, and I'm proud I did that! A few years ago I might not have

even tried! Some people would be too scared to even do what I did."

You can also extend this to others around you:

"Ah, he might be taking a break now, but I'm sure he worked hard. It's his job to keep himself on track anyways!"

"She keeps getting better, and that's awesome."

If you notice yourself having many judgmental thoughts, record the following in your journal:

1. Who were the thoughts about, you or others?

2. Why do you think you had this thought?

3. Is the thought helpful, or hurtful?

4. If the thought was hurtful, what positive alternative can you say instead?

Judgment of us and others just puts more negative energy into the world and creates unnecessary drama. Everybody is on their own journey and will figure things out. It's good to help others out by suggesting possible ways they can improve themselves, **but just because they don't do things at 100% efficiency doesn't mean they are inherently bad. Just because someone doesn't do something the way you think they should doesn't mean they are worthless.**

If we accept that we—and everyone else out there (besides hardened criminals)—are good people, and accept them as they are, then everything we tell them, we give to them as a gift. One of the fundamental problems in relationships is that people cannot accept each other as they are, and expect change.

This is a recipe for disaster.

You should want people to change to be happier, but not because there is something fundamentally wrong with them. This goes for yourself too. Learn to keep improving to become better, but not because there is something bad about you. In fact, you have a great drive to share amazing work, words, and feelings to the world, and that's what drives you to do the best you can.

Chapter 28.
Procrastination

"Let me just check my Facebook quick."
"Oh man, they released a new YouTube clip!"

We all procrastinate, to some extent. There's something that we've been meaning to do for A LONG time, but we just don't want to do it.

Maybe it's an annoying errand, going to the gym, or something more important.

But why? Why can't we just get that thing done?

Why You Might Do It and Where It Comes From

Everyone prefers instant gratification over hard work.

When you complete a task, you get a release of dopamine in your brain as a reward. You feel good, confident, and happy. But checking Facebook, Reddit, your smart phone, and all that other time-wasting stuff (that I spend so much time on, argh!) elicits dopamine hits too...and unfortunately, it's FAR easier to open your Internet browser and type in a few letters or click the power button than it is to go to the gym[1].

It's one of the reasons why I loved going without a cell phone for two months after reading about all the issues associated with technology. You can learn more about that here.[2]

Going to the gym might suck, but sometimes you procrastinate

116

on things that seem "scary." Or, you trick yourself into thinking that they aren't important. This could range from calling your family or a romantic interest, to applying to new jobs, to leaving the current job you hate, to going to therapy.

"I'll do it later."

"I'm too busy right now."

Sound familiar?

What's the Positive Alternative to Boost Your Mental Energy?

When it comes to procrastination, it's usually not that you don't have time or don't want to, it's that you:

1. Have not broken down what you need to do into small, actionable steps. Your mind sees the totality of a task to be done. So if I had "Write a book" as an action item, it would NEVER be written.

2. Are scared about doing something. You put it off because it makes you feel nervous. It's easier to do nothing than to take a risk.

3. Allow **perfectionism** (see Chapter 27) to creep in. It's easier to procrastinate then risk something being judged as "low quality."

If your brain thinks a task is monumental and large, it will NEVER let you do it. It will occupy itself with other things in the meantime, creating busy work for you, and the important stuff will never get done.

If your brain thinks something is too scary, then you will just distract and numb yourself from doing that thing.

"Someday is not a day of the week."

A bit of procrastination never hurt anyone, but it can be very serious. I unknowingly put off my dating life for years due to fears of dealing with women. Even now I sometimes do it, though deep inside I know that I want to hang out with cool girls. Why do I do it? Because I know I have fears from my past.

But imagine what would have happened if I had gotten very old without experiencing ANY dating. *"Where did all my time go?"* I would say. *"I always meant to do it..."*

You always mean to do those important things, but never do. It sucks.

So you must learn to face your fears (see **fear**, Chapter 20), and properly break things down so that your brain doesn't think they are huge, monumental tasks. You must also learn to reward yourself when you do something good.

Your internal desire sometimes isn't enough to get things done. As much as you would like to think that if you say you will do something, then it will happen, sometimes you need external things pushing you. That's where using deadlines and outside penalties comes in.

Practical Exercises

Curbing procrastination, and specifically productivity, is a large topic that I could write a separate book on, but here are some helpful tips:

Think about something you've been putting off, such as an errand, going to the gym, dating, etc. Talk to a trusted person and ask them if they think you are putting it off due to fear, laziness, or busying yourself with unimportant items. Try to be honest with yourself as well. Then:

If it's **fear**: You build courage by facing fear. You get it AFTER facing it, not before. So you must do what you are scared of, and, as you continuously push through fear, it will become easier and easier. If it's a small thing, do it **now**. Have that friend help you through it if you need to. If you feel that it's a bigger issue or will take longer, read through the section on **fear**, Chapter 20, and move forward to face what's bothering you by breaking it down into small, manageable steps.

If it's **laziness** on a certain item, you need to suck it up and do it. Free yourself from the stress and aggravation of NOT doing it and just get it done so you can move on to the next thing. Some ideas:

1. Tell a friend that you will do the thing by a certain date, and if you do not, you have to pay them a certain amount of money. This way you are forced to get it done.

2. You can give yourself a reward when you finish the task, such as going out for coffee, ice cream, taking an hour off of work, etc.

If you are busying yourself with unimportant items, chances are that the task is far too large and your brain does not see how you can do it. If I did not break this book down into bite-size writing portions, how would I EVER get it done?! *"Hey Noam, I want you to write a book in three months. OK? Cool."*

WHAT?!

To write this book, I broke it down into the smallest steps I could. Here's a broad overview:

•   Brainstorm ideas of what to write about.

•   Pick one I am most passionate about.

•   Brainstorm an outline/create the table of contents.

- Brainstorm the mental wastes I want to write about.

- Write in 30-minute chunks during the day, 1-2 times a day.

- Edit the book.

- Hire a copy editor.

- Decide on a title.

- Convert the book into publishable formats.

- Publish.

These major milestones were further broken down into sub-goals, and each had a date assigned to it so that I was keeping myself on track. If you've heard of S.M.A.R.T. goals, that's what you should be aiming for.

The process is:

1. **Determine what you want to do.**

2. **Break it down into the smallest action steps you need to. Be SPECIFIC. Ask yourself what you need to do to get this accomplished.**

3. **Determine a deadline for each task.**

For example, let's say you have been procrastinating on finding a girlfriend or boyfriend. You aren't scared, you just have no idea what to do.

Well you need to go to social events or places to meet people. Then you need to ask people for their contact information. Then you need to go on dates.

See how breaking it down makes it easier, and you can actually see the end in sight?

You can get specific, saying: "Go to two social events a week,"

"Talk to five people at each event," etc.

This also applies to a more boring type of goal, such as taking the car in to get fixed:

- Pick a day when I want to take the car in.

- E-mail my boss that I will be an hour late for work because of taking the car in, but I will work back the hour overtime at night.

- Let my family know that I will be taking the car in that day and that they cannot use it.

- Take the car in.

This may seem boring and unsexy—and it is—but it also makes sure you get your stuff done. The less brainpower you use in the moment, the less resistance there is, and the more things get done. Period.

As I mentioned, using deadlines and penalties as external motivation forces you to **ACT**. They can be useful if you perpetually procrastinate. Equally important are rewards, such as a new book, or even just telling yourself "*Great job!*" Rewards for productivity and getting things accomplished trigger your brain into saying, "*If I get this done, I get something and feel good. So let me do this thing!*"

I was procrastinating most recently on buying my ticket to Asia (due to fear). So, after a few weeks of this, I told my friend that I'd book it by next week or I'd clean his room and do his laundry.

The ticket got booked, thankfully.

Passive Methods for Curbing Procrastination

If you have huge issues with using technology or websites to not do work, here are some suggestions:

1. Turn off your phone and e-mail notifications during the workday.

2. Download a program or extension like *StayFocusd*, which lets you block certain websites or ALL Internet traffic at specific hours. It can also allow you a certain number of minutes per day on websites like Reddit and YouTube.

3. If you are going to watch YouTube, work for 20 or 30 minutes then give yourself a reward of 5 minutes of YouTube. This is far better than wasting hours getting nothing done.

Accomplishing things frees up time to do what you want. Productive people are happy people. Join the happy crowd and write your own book...and send me a copy please.

---

[1] Weinschenk, Susan. *Why We're All Addicted to Texts, Twitter and Google*. Psychology Today. Retrieved from www.psychologytoday.com/blog/brain-wise/201209/why-were-all-addicted-texts-twitter- and-google on January 7th, 2015.

[2] See: http://lightwayofthinking.com/technology-anxiety-and-depression-why-i-loved-going-without-a- cell-phone-for-two-months-and-other-technology-fast-experiments/

Chapter 29.
Self-Criticism and Negative Self-Talk

"I suck."
"I'll never get this right."
"I haven't done enough."
"Why am I such a loser?"

One of the longest blog posts I ever wrote was about how bullying affects a person's self-esteem. In case you are interested, there is a link to the blog post at the end of this chapter. I was bullied all throughout elementary school, for eight years, and this implanted a critical voice inside my head that told me I was never good enough, and that I sucked.

Good thing I'm learning to ignore this more and more, because life and I are both too awesome to waste time in negativity.

Why You Might Do It and Where It Comes From

Usually some traumas from the past caused you to have a bad opinion of yourself, or you were constantly put down by authority figures and those that surrounded you.

Examples include:

- Being bullied.

- Having overly critical parents.

- Being abused or constantly reprimanded by parents or

authority figures.

In all of these examples, the messages you receive would all be grounded in shame: *"There's something wrong with me," "I'm bad," "What did I do wrong? I just want to make people happy and be happy myself."* If these messages come from authority figures, or a group, then perhaps you start to believe that there is something wrong with you. I mean, bigger people know more than you, right? And if so many people tell you that you are bad, they must be correct, right?

Once this translates into adulthood, confidence is shot down, dating and relating to the opposite sex is taken to an EXTREME degree (rejection), and the continuous stream of negative thoughts pounds you into the ground.

What's the Positive Alternative to Boost Your Mental Energy?

When faced with people who don't like them, people with high self-esteem and self-confidence would either say:

"Oh well, can't be liked by everyone. I like me!"

Or they would consult within their own intuition and trusted friends to see if they really WERE doing something bad.

But they trust their own opinions more than others, and are not moved by what other people are saying.

A thought experiment worth trying is to ask:

"What if I didn't pay attention to any of the negative thoughts saying I was bad?"

What if you just let them pass. What if you kept telling yourself that, hey, it's OK, you did your best. What if you bathed yourself in self-love?

OK, I admit that was a bit hippyish, but the point is that those with high self-esteem and self-confidence treat themselves well, and talk to themselves in a kind way. Criticism and wanting to be better is fine, as long as they are both constructive forces in your life, not destructive forces making you feel like crap.

Practical Exercises

- ### Gratitude Exercise and Practice

See **jealousy and envy**, Chapter 26.

- ### I Am My Own Best Friend

I am going to assume that you are not a complete asshole, and that when a friend comes to you in need, crying or depressed, you console them and try to help them out. You speak kindly to them.

Why is it that we are so kind to our friends, but so mean to and hard on ourselves?

For the next two weeks, anytime you hear yourself being mean when something occurs, try being kind with positive self-talk. Always tell yourself that it's OK, you can do it, you are amazing and getting better every day.

Fill in the following table in your journal for at least one event a day:

Day	Event	Negative/ Critical Thought	What I Said to Be Kind to Myself Instead

After this week, write down how you feel about being kind to yourself. Does it feel different, weird, better, worse? How do you want to proceed from now on?

You can't control negative thoughts from happening. We established that at the beginning of this book. But you can control how much energy and validity you give to them.

- ### **Doing Things for Myself**

Many times we spend our days JUST doing work, or things for other people. We are reacting and trying to make everyone happy, but there is no time left over for us.

Spend at least 20 minutes each day this week doing something just for you—something that you love. That could be going to the gym, playing an instrument, watching an amazing show, etc. Whatever it is, just do it because it is for you.

- ### **Taking Compliments Fully, and Compliments Document**

Those with poor self-esteem usually cannot accept compliments directly. Usually, they think that the person is being overly friendly, that they want something, or add a qualifier. For example:

"You did an awesome job on that report!"

"Thanks...**BUT** it was a bit rushed and I bet I could do better."

"You're a good-looking guy."

"Aw shucks, thanks for saying that. **I still think** I need to get some better clothes though, I've been meaning to go shopping for a while."

For the next week, you are NOT allowed to qualify any

compliment.

You are only allowed to respond with "Thank you" and a smile. Feel the weight of the positive energy this person is giving you and take it in. Yes, you might not be perfect. Yes, you can always improve. But you are pretty good right now, and this person is telling you that. Embrace it!

Go ahead and ask your friends and maybe even your family what your positive qualities are. Tell them it's for an exercise taking stock of the positive traits people recognize in you. What do they say?

In your journal, note down what people have said about you. I have a "**compliments document**" with a collection of nice things people have said about me that I can always look at when I feel down. It reminds me about my positive traits. I might feel a bit down on myself one day, but then I'll read how my friends said I was really emotionally aware of myself and others, or girls I dated saying I was sexy and handsome, or people saying I had helped them through some tough times and they really appreciated it...then I feel a lot better.

You may also try putting these compliments throughout your house and room on Post-it notes so that there is positive energy everywhere. It's hard to be depressed when you keep seeing reminders of the good things people say about you.

Add things to your list as well. Ask yourself:

- What do I really appreciate about myself?

- What am I really good at?

- What kind of things have I been successful at doing?

- What traits do I have that I know people would desire?

Maybe you are really intelligent, play the guitar, can bring people together, are caring, work hard, etc. Whatever you have going for you, bring this to the forefront of your mind and remind yourself of your positive attributes. Everyone has strengths and weaknesses, and we can always improve, but so often we forget all the amazing things we can do. Remind yourself everyday if you need to!

In the one life you have, strive to be kind to yourself. You will be happier, less anxious, more understanding, and EVEN see yourself being kinder and more empathetic to others.

<u>Link to bullying article</u>:

<u>http://lightwayofthinking.com/bullying/</u>

Chapter 30.
Blame

"I can't stand my dad—he always yells at me."
"I should have a job already so I can move out. It's the economy's fault."

It's always somebody else's fault.

Many times, due to anger, frustration, or not wanting negative feelings, we blame others.

Your parents are responsible for you being broke because they didn't teach you life skills.

Your friends are responsible for you feeling lonely.

The opposite sex is responsible for the fact that you have no dates.

Everyone is mean—that's why they walk all over you.

Or:

Did your parents do as good of a job as they could, and now it's up to you to learn how to take your life where it needs to go?

Are your friends there for you and all you need to do is ask for support?

Is the opposite sex waiting for you—you just need to go to social events and TALK to people?

Is it your job to be assertive, tell people to stop when they are being mean, remove them from your life, or learn how to be less sensitive to what people say?

Is it actually all under **YOUR** control, and is it all **YOUR** fault?

Why You Might Do It and Where It Comes From

Negative emotions suck, and it'd be awesome to get rid of them. Placing blame on others is a convenient way to do this.

Instead of accepting responsibility for needing to change something in your life, you say someone else should do it for you, or you think things should happen without having to put in any work.

This perpetuates a victim mentality that hurts you. You're powerless, everyone else is in control, and you can't do anything.

Sometimes, you can't control what happens to you. Especially when you are young, you can be defenseless in very bad situations.

What's the Positive Alternative to Boost Your Mental Energy?

Now that you are an adult, it's time to take responsibility for everything.

Perhaps it's not fair that you got bullied when you were a kid—you didn't know better. But it is your responsibility now to find ways to build up your self-esteem and find people who support you.

You might not have had any dates in the past, but it's up to you to learn how to communicate effectively with the opposite sex, meet people, and go on dates.

You might be a more anxious person than some, but it's up to you to find resources like this book to help you, go to therapy, and go on meditation retreats.

When you start accepting that everything is under your control, you feel AMAZING. You are no longer powerless. It doesn't mean that things come easy—you still need to put in work. It doesn't mean that you can control EVERYTHING. But a lot more is possible than if you gave everyone the power to decide how your life will unfold.

It's true that you cannot control OUTSIDE circumstances and events that happen in life, but you can control your reactions to what happens.

You can control your desires and dreams and the amount of work you put in to get there. To paraphrase one of the best quotes my dad has told me, dreams or goals are constructed of 1% inspiration and 99% perspiration.

Stop blaming others, accept that you need to put work in, and get what you want.

Practical Exercises

Any time you feel yourself blaming others, stop. Answer the following:

- Who are you blaming?

- Why are you blaming them/what do you think they are doing?

- What emotion do you feel right now? Anger, frustration, sadness?

- Consider the possibility that it might be on YOU to fix the issue. What do you think you could do to help yourself? Or, why is something going wrong for you?

Journaling and Accountability

When you feel yourself starting to blame someone, answer the questions above. If an action is required, write down steps to achieve what you are frustrated about.

For example:

"It's all girls' faults I have no dates" -> "It's on me to go out and meet more girls" -> "I need to go to two social events a week and say hi to at least three girls at each."

"It's my parents fault I feel like such crap living at home" -> "It's on me to make the decision to move out" -> "I need to take a part-time job to earn money so I can move out by X date."

If you need to, tell someone about the steps you need to take and give them the deadlines you will accomplish them by.

By doing this, you are turning wasted blame energy into actionable steps to create the life you want. Stop giving others power over your life and take charge.

Chapter 31.
Pessimism, Negative Thinking, and Limiting Beliefs

"He won't like me, there's no point."
"I probably won't have fun, I should just stay home."
"It's a waste of time."

A large problem that many of us suffer from—and a large symptom of depression—is being pessimistic, or thinking negatively. You think there's no point, you'll probably fail, why even try...

If you thought this way for everything, would you ever try ANYTHING?

If you are always **WORRIED** that something bad will happen and it prevents you from doing anything, are you even living? You're in a cage surrounded by your fears. In fact, your fears are the bars holding you in.

And that sucks!

Why You Might Do It and Where It Comes From

Many things can cause you to think negatively. If you are used to bad things happening to you and nothing working out, never seeing the amazing things that are happening right in front of you, not knowing how to be grateful...you're in for a rough ride.

In psychology there is a phenomenon known as

confirmation bias. Typically, one applies it in decision making: You are trying to make a decision but have an emotional investment (that's why you're struggling with a decision) and are already biased. For example, whether to break up with someone you're seeing. You might already think you should, but wonder if you're making the wrong decision. Or, you might really like the person, but perhaps they're bad for you.

Without knowing it, you will regard the information SUPPORTING your emotion as having more meaning. You will try to find people that will give you the support you need.

You can read more about confirmation bias and how to cut it off here.[1]

When we apply this to your outlook on life, it would go like this:

When you EXPECT negative things to happen, and you think all life is bad, you will automatically self-select reasons why life is bad: You're single and can't find anyone, you're not as in shape as you want to be, your friends bug you sometimes, your family nags you, and so on.

This is not to say that some of this stuff is not true. I mean, my family and friends can drive me nuts sometimes...but then, you are missing all the good parts of life.

What's the Positive Alternative to Boost Your Mental Energy?

All it takes is a tiny bit of work, re-framing your perspective, and some patience, and you can be living a FAR better life while becoming incredibly happy.

For example, instead of looking at how your friends and family drive you nuts, you can think about how they are always there for you and provide you with support. Your family did their best to raise you, and spent thousands of dollars investing in your future. They taught you as best they could.

You might be single, sure—but there are PLENTY of opportunities to meet people and not be single. You can enjoy the extra time you have now to pursue things you want in life, but still keep looking for partners.

You might not be the most fit, but there are HUNDREDS of ways to exercise and get in shape. There are plenty of free online tools that give you workout routines if you don't want to pay. Or, there are plenty of personal trainers who would gladly help you reach your goals.

As Mark Manson would say, "*Shut up and be grateful.*[2]"

So yes, sometimes bad things happen. That's life. But many of us spend hours focusing on all the negatives instead of the positives. Or, we focus on minute negative things because they bug us more, and disregard all the positives that we take for granted—having food, friends, family to call on, the ability to change our lives if we put in some work, etc.

It doesn't matter what happened to you, or what your situation is. The question is, what are you going to do about it? You control your reactions to all that happens around you, so start focusing on all the good, opportunity, and help that is out there. You just need to go out, find it, and grab it.

I had extreme social anxiety from being bullied and assuming everything would go wrong. I always assumed people were out to get me—that they didn't like me—and I still suffer a lot from these issues every day. But in working hard and trying to see things from a more positive perspective, I have become a lot happier. I'm not perfect, but far far better. If I can do it, so can you.

Limiting Beliefs

The other part of the story is focusing on your **beliefs**.

As we grow up we are programmed with beliefs, each person having a unique set. I mean, why is it that some really handsome guy feels nervous around women whereas another guy who might be less attractive physically is free flowing and says whatever he wants? They each have their own beliefs that can hurt or help them.

Beliefs that hurt you are typically referred to as **limiting beliefs**, and they prevent you from living the life you want. They are another form of constriction caging you in.

The nice thing about beliefs is that just as they have been programmed into you, they can be de-programmed, or vice versa.

To take an **EXTREME** example, most people are familiar with the fact that the Nazis persecuted and killed over six million Jews during World War II.

Prior to their incarceration and persecution, the Jews were normal people with jobs. They felt entitled and important, being doctors, lawyers, and so on. But then, as the Nazis came into power, the Jews were partially used as scapegoats for the loss of German pride after World War I. Non-Jewish Germans were programmed with the belief that "Jews are bad," and with constant persecution leading to concentration camps full of humiliation, brutality, and unfair working conditions, how could the Jewish people not believe "I am terrible." Unless, of course, they had extremely strong wills to help them push through, and their beliefs and faith were not shaken.[3]

Again, this is an EXTREME example. But it is possible, due to bullying, trauma, abuse, and so on, that you may have some less extreme "I am bad" beliefs in you.

How can you begin to de-program these hurtful beliefs?

Practical Exercises

- ### <u>Being Grateful</u>

The gratitude exercise in the **jealousy and envy** section, Chapter 26, will really help focus your mind on all the good things you have right now.

- ### <u>Biofeedback and the Rubber Band</u>

As a way of conditioning your mind to disregard pessimistic or negative thoughts, you can use a rubber band around your wrist. Anytime you hear a negative thought, acknowledge it, snap the rubber band, and replace the thought with a positive one. By doing this, you are training your body and mind that a negative thought is associated with pain, so why would it bother with them? Combine this with the next exercise...

- ### <u>Replace Negative Thoughts with Positive Variants</u>

Again, this is not to say that you will NEVER have a negative thought. But, you will learn to let them pass ever more frequently, and focus on positive thoughts.

When you hear a negative thought, say, *"OK, but..."* and think of the positive options. Then continue about your day. Don't let your mind bring you down.

For example:

"I'm ugly, nobody wants me."

"OK, but I can go to the gym to look better for me. I can get some new clothes, I can ask my friends to help me dress better...and I know that I have a lot going for me inside too (name things you love about yourself)! Huh, doesn't make sense then, since I can do something about this!"

"I hate my life."

"OK, but I have awesome friends, a good family, I'm smart... If there's something I don't like, I should probably work on it instead of **complaining**. I've got a lot right now anyways, I mean, I'm not starving or dying of thirst... and some people don't even have food or water. I've had some beautiful moments (have you ever loved, traveled, felt alive, done something most people cannot do, etc.?). Wow, life's pretty great. I can always make it better, but it's pretty good right now!"

This will take practice, but it's worth it.

In your journal, you will answer the following questions:

- What negative thought did you have?

- How did it make you feel?

- What can you say that's positive instead? (Think hard, this may involve some creativity on your part. Some things aren't as easy as changing "I suck" to "I'm OK.")

- How does thinking about the positive make you feel (instead of thinking about the negative)?

- What would you rather focus on?

For example:

- "I'm a terrible person, I can't do anything right."

- I feel like I'm worthless, sad, lonely, and angry.

- I could say, "I'm always getting better every day, I'm trying to improve myself. I know I have some positive qualities."

- Instead, I now feel like I'm being kinder to myself. I feel energized because I'm working WITH myself instead of beating myself down. I prefer focusing on the positive thought.

• __De-programming Limiting Beliefs__

It will take some introspection and self-awareness to know what limiting beliefs you have. I cannot know without talking to you one-on-one what might be going on inside your noggin. But some common ones may be:

- *"I am bad."*

- *"People don't like me."*

- *"I can't do it."*

- *"I'm going to fail if I do X."*

I usually break belief programming into two steps, which build upon each other:

1. **You can assume a belief is true.**

2. **You can find proof to contradict a current belief and replace it with a new one.**

If a belief is programmed inside, you can easily assume the opposite. I mean, why not experiment? Instead of thinking that people are all scary and out to get you, what if you instead thought that people wanted to help you? How would that affect how you carry yourself in life or approach people? What if you assumed people wanted intimacy and connection just as much as you did?

Focusing on **ONE BELIEF AT A TIME** in certain situations can reveal some interesting results. Treat it like a science experiment!

When aiming to change a belief, you will need at least two weeks to do your experiment, and most likely longer (perhaps YEARS) if it's really deep. But the point is that this will get you going on the right path.

Fill in the following information in your journal:

- What belief do you have right now that you want to change?

- What are you assuming instead?

- How might you go about testing your assumption? How can you prove to yourself that the belief is real?

- Everyday - What did you find today? How did you feel holding the new belief? What happened?

Doing this may be enough to convince you that "Hey, this makes more sense and feels better, I should just stick with it!" By testing your assumption in life, you are also gathering proof to provide your brain with evidence that your old, hurtful belief is probably false.

Sometimes, our brains really need a well-ordered way to gather proof of a belief being false. For example, you could go out and assume people are friendly, then see what happens when you talk to people. OK.

But what about deeper beliefs, such as "*I am unlovable?*"

I challenge you to go through your past to find out times when you were given love. I used to hold that belief, and it sometimes creeps in still, but then I use my brain to think back to the past when people loved me—or even right now, when people love me:

My friends tell me they love me all the time, even after I make mistakes.

- My family tells me they love me.

- My family spent thousands raising me, taking me to activities and on trips, and letting me do activities like martial arts—and that's pretty awesome.

- I've had girlfriends who tried to be there for me when I asked, and told me that they loved me.

- People give me their time when I'm in trouble and feel bad, and that must mean they care.

- So while I have not set out a PLAN to prove that people love me, I have gathered evidence to show that it is true.

- **"Catch and Release"**

One of the primary causes of anxiety and depression is believing, listening to, or giving in to negative and hurtful thoughts. You might give a positive *"I'm good"* thought a cursory listen, but you pay so much attention when you hear *"I suck, I'm a failure."* Why is this?

You formed a habit as you were growing up, to listen to these thoughts. But through these exercises you will break that habit. One of the best ways to do this is via "catch and release."

For two weeks you practice hearing all negative thoughts, not pushing them down, yet not continuously **churning** (Chapter 24) on them and giving them energy. Just like something that lives, if you don't give it food, fuel, or energy, the thought dies. That's our goal.

Of course, if you have been a slave to negative thoughts for your entire life, this will be EXTREMELY difficult and you probably will still churn on a few. But the point is to get used to letting them go, and realizing that if you are not your mind (which is creating the thoughts), you don't have to believe them and can be kind to yourself instead.

Ignoring and letting negative thoughts and beliefs pass while also continually focusing on the positive is one of the KEY skills in increasing your positive mood and self-esteem.

Don't expect this to be an overnight change if you've always thought negatively before. This, along with almost ALL the exercises in this book, takes time to implement. But once you do, you will be reaping the benefits for your entire life.

I wish you happiness.

---

[1] See: http://lightwayofthinking.com/confirmation-bias-emotions-screwing-over/

[2] Manson, Mark. *Shut Up and Be Grateful.* markmanson.net. Retrieved from http://markmanson.net/shut-up-and-be-grateful on January 7th, 2015.

[3] Viktor Frankl's book, *Man's Search for Meaning*, is an outstanding and truly memorable read about his experiences surviving the Holocaust. In it, he discusses his theory of logotherapy - his theory that a person can live and survive extreme circumstances so long as they have something to believe in and keep living for. For him - it was the fact that he may see his wife one day again. I highly suggest reading it for inspiration.

Chapter 32.
Guessing What Someone Is Thinking About You and Trying to Please Others

"What if they don't like me?"
"I shouldn't do that or they'll be mad."
"I hope this makes her happy."

In Dr. Robert Glover's book *No More Mr. Nice Guy*,[1] he discusses how nice guys (NGs) hate feeling anxious, so they do a whole bunch of ridiculous things to be relieved of their anxiety and make people like them. The problem for these guys is that when they try to make someone like them, they may be putting others' needs above theirs. And if you always feel the need to please someone, where and when does it stop?

For example, a NG may let his wife vent to or nag him just so that him saying "Stop" doesn't make her angry. He assumes he knows what will happen and what she will think. He is also trying to please her by being good and listening to her when really he doesn't care or feel like hearing her in that moment.

Not only is this not fair to her (because he's not actually giving her his attention), but he's also hurting the relationship by building up a passive aggressive hate of her actions.

Not good.

And while I use nice <u>GUY</u> syndrome, this can also be readily applied to women. For instance, when a girl stays with a guy in a non-committed relationship to keep the guy around and happy (when what she TRULY wants is a monogamous and long-term boyfriend):

Needs are pushed down.

People get sad and angry.

And everyone loses—even the person you think you are helping.

Why You Might Do It and Where It Comes From

There are many reasons why you might want to guess how someone feels about you, or please them. Sure, naturally we all want people to like us. This is human nature. But when you start micro-analyzing everything that is said to make sure you aren't harming anyone, and everything is hunky dorey...

You get into a realm of neediness.

Mark Manson defined neediness in his book *Models* as prioritizing someone else's needs over yours.

In other words, being a people pleaser.

Somewhere along the line, you learned that it wasn't OK to assert your own needs, and that something bad might happen if you say "No." You never developed something inside to ask yourself "*What do I want?*" but only learned that if you were to be thought of as good, you needed to ensure that everyone else is happy...even if that means making yourself absolutely miserable.

Some examples:

• An overly critical father who says you could always do more, and, as much as you try, you can never live up to his standards.

• A mother with pent up emotions and no one to let them out to, so you become her source of support. Your needs are pushed aside for hers.

The other thing you must realize is that by trying to please others, you are trying to take care of their needs for them. We all have needs, from relationships, to health, to money and so on. When we are kids, it is up to our parents to help us get these needs met. But when we grow up to be adults, our needs get more complicated (a kid doesn't care about his "life purpose"), and we must get them met on our own. The needs may INVOLVE others (intimacy needs met through your girlfriend or boyfriend), but we are responsible for finding that significant other (going on dates, learning how to talk to people, etc.).

Trying to ensure that others' needs are met for them is not only EXTREMELY stressful for you (I mean, you already have to take care of YOURSELF!). It's nearly impossible to read what a person wants at all times.

This also applies to expressing emotions. It is someone else's responsibility to express if they feel frustrated, sad, angry, etc. towards you or any other person. It is not your job to figure things out.

What's the Positive Alternative to Boost Your Mental Energy?

A three-point answer:

1. Realize that humans are EXTREMELY complex and you have absolutely no control over what someone thinks of you. You can try to make everyone happy, but will be exhausted, pulled every which way, and there's no universal guide called "Do X and every person will like you." There are some guidelines, of course (people usually prefer if you don't walk up to them and call them an asshole), but what you do for one person may irritate the hell out of someone else. Hence, the only logical conclusion is to be yourself, and to draw closer to people who

like you for being you.

2.   It is each person's responsibility to get their own needs met and express dissatisfaction.

3.   You can only be aware of how you think and feel about yourself and others. If that is the case, then you can only try to **please yourself,** because you know 100% of the time what you are thinking.

As you become happier with yourself and your life, you start to carve out this amazing feature of you where you are 100% yourself in front of everyone you meet. You are more like a kid with no filters on your words or actions. Your beliefs change from "*I hope they like me*" to "*I wonder if they are cool and can add something to my life?*" and your neediness plummets. Your boundaries become stronger as well.[2]

As this change happens, you find yourself becoming happier and happier, because the people you surround yourself with are more of whom you like to be around, without any BS of trying to make them happy.

And sure, sometimes even these people will become angry or frustrated with you. Maybe you did do something silly, stupid, or worth those feelings. But, because you care more about these people that are close to you, you will be able to decide if you should work things out and apologize. They will, in turn, hopefully be willing to listen to you and give you feedback while expressing what they want directly without any drama.

Focus on making yourself happy first. You're the only person that you can make happy 100% of the time.

When it comes to getting needs met, there may be times when you do something for someone as a gift (i.e., perhaps it violates what you want, or your boundaries, but you do it because you care for them, love them, and are not doing it out of fear). This is absolutely fine. The problem is when you do things for someone because you are afraid of them being angry at you, or they are bullying you into it.

There is also nothing bad about asking someone, *"What's wrong?"* or being empathetic. Again, as long as it's out of genuine concern and not to make them less angry at you.

Practical Exercises

The practical exercises for this particular section are a bit challenging, as the "neediness" mentality is something that declines as you do more for yourself and try to improve life **JUST FOR YOU**. In fact, by reading this book, you are taking a good step along this path.

- **<u>Doing Things for Myself</u>**

See the exercise in the **self-criticism and negative self-talk** section, Chapter 29.

- **<u>Bucket List</u>**

This is a really fun activity that increases your self-esteem. Many people have a level of neediness because they are not doing things they want to do in their life, or they have no idea where they are going. A "bucket list" is a list of items you would like to accomplish in your life.

Or, as *The Buried Life* would ask:

"What do you want to do before you die?"

Take a sheet of paper, or several sheets. Set a timer for 10 minutes and answer this question. Don't stop writing.

It could look like this:

1. Write a book.

2. See the pyramids.

3. Get married.

4. Learn about tantric sex.

5. Go lawn bowling.

6. Etc.

Whatever things you want to try in life, put them down. Go nuts! This is your time to shine!

After 10 minutes of writing, take one thing on that list and create some action steps to accomplish it THIS WEEK. It can be something small (I have "playing chess in the park" as a bucket list item), but anything that gets you closer to living the life you want.

As you cross off more things on your bucket list, you will feel happier and have a higher self-esteem because you are out exploring the world, and accomplishing things just for you.

You might even consider getting a really nice notebook to keep your list in...that's what I have.

- **<u>Take Notice and Soothe</u>**

When people get frustrated or angry, or raise their voice at you, how do you feel and what action do you take?

For one week, note down instances where you feel compelled to take an action, even when you don't want to, to make someone happy or get them off your back.

Fill in the following:

- When did the event take place?

- Who were you talking to?

- What did they want you to do?

- How do you think they were feeling at that moment towards

you?

- What did you actually want to do?

- What did you end up doing? And why?

- How does the action you took make you feel?

- Do you really think you can predict how someone feels and how doing something will make them feel?

- Has this pattern happened before? (I.e., this person feels a certain way and you have to respond somehow?)

- If a pattern keeps repeating where you take action you do not want to because you are afraid of the person being angry, it is time to practice **self-soothing**.

In *No More Mr. Nice Guy*, Dr. Glover discusses how people who are really good at handling their anxiety self-soothe all the time. They tell themselves that things will be OK, they will handle it, they are only responsible for their feelings, and so on.

You need to practice this.

For the next unsettling event that happens with this person, when you find yourself feeling worried about them being upset, stand your ground when it comes to what you want to do. Keep telling yourself *"I can handle this person feeling bad towards me," "I can only take care of my needs,"* and *"I will handle it."*

If you need more support, talk to a friend, counselor, or trusted figure about feeling bullied by another person or putting their needs first. Tell them you will stand up to them next time and let them hold you accountable.

Trying to please others and guessing what others are thinking of you comes down to:

1. Neediness and self-esteem.

2.   Boundaries.

3.   Recognizing that each person is responsible for their needs only.

Neediness drops and self-esteem rises when you move your life in the direction you want, and do things just for you. This helps you establish stronger boundaries, while learning how to say "no."

As you set stronger boundaries, you realize that it is up to another person to let you know if they want something, and that trying to predict what they need all the time is tiresome, frustrating, and useless.

---

[1] One of the most life changing books I've read. It's incredibly short at around 150 pages, but it packs a punch. I recommend all men read it, and perhaps women too to make sure that your guy doesn't suffer from Nice Guy Syndrome, or to alert him of it.

[2] A good book and guide to read for techniques on setting boundaries is the classic *When I Say No, I Feel Guilty* by Dr. Manuel J. Smith.

Chapter 33.
Assuming the Present Will Never Change and Over-Identifying With It

"I'm always going to feel this way!"
"I don't want this to ever end!"
"I'll always be alone."

You learned about the **Law of Nature** in the introduction, which states that all things arise just to pass away.

- You were born, but one day you will die.You are in a relationship, but one day it will end, either due to an argument or clash that is unsolvable, or due to the other person passing.

- An event begins, but then has to end.

- A trip does not last forever.

- But this also applies to emotions:

- You don't ALWAYS feel ecstatic or happy, sometimes you just feel "normal."

- And on the flip side, sometimes you just feel sad.

The problem comes when you over-identify with the present and either push it away (you are averse to it) or wish it would never stop (cling to it). All moments in life are meant to eventually end, and it is this knowledge that helps everyone move through life with more peace.

Why You Might Do It and Where It Comes From

It's possible that if your amygdala was triggered a large number of times in childhood, that you are used to extremely jarring events in the present that seem like a huge deal. If that's the case, then you worry about those things repeating, as you needed to expend so much energy to prevent them from overtaking you. In this sense, it's like a warning system trying to prevent the present from lasting too long.

Typically, if you have not had a great deal of practice using your logical brain to talk to your emotional brain and believe all of your emotions, you will have issues with this mental waste. When I say, "Believe all of your emotions," I mean that you fully let them take you over to the point where you can no longer override them with logic. You can feel angry, but that doesn't mean that you let the anger compel you to punch a brick wall...as much as you may want to.

Of course, nothing lasts forever, and it's usually not that big of a deal.

The "always" parts of the thoughts above should trigger an alarm in your brain. Remember, all things arise to pass away. Believing these thoughts is ignoring the fundamental **Law of Nature**: Things cannot last forever. We usually buy into these thoughts when we are feeling deep emotions of sadness, loneliness, regret, anger, and frustration.

What's the Positive Alternative to Boost Your Mental Energy?

The positive alternative, again, is to realize that all things will end, and to not push things away or repress them.

By engaging the logical brain to talk to your emotional one, you can begin to realize how false "always" thoughts are.

For example: You break up with your significant other and you have a thought: "*I'll always be single, I'll never find someone else.*" Well chances are (speaking from personal experience) you might have also had this thought before meeting your last partner, so already this thought is flawed. Moreover, after a time of being OK with being single, if you start talking to people and going to social events, pushing yourself to ask people on dates, do you really think you'll never meet ANYONE?

Our emotions come from our mental workup and pasts, and in a different situation someone else might have felt completely differently. Someone else might say, "*We had a great time, and I can't wait to meet someone else and have an adventure with them!*" Once you realize that your reactions to your thoughts and emotions are extremely personal and nobody will ever feel the exact same way in an identical situation, you can begin to look at things more objectively.

So if you feel sad, that's OK. Look at life overall and think about all the wondrous things around you, from the very simple to the very complex, and know that you'll be happy again. Don't repress your sadness, feel it fully (the exercises in this section will help in learning how to "feel" emotions).

If you're happy and enjoying an event, do so fully. Just know in your mind that eventually the moment will end, so you might as well be as present as you can to enjoy it to your utmost ability.

This is a very simple concept that ALL of us have incredible difficulty with. It's really easy to enjoy something awesome, but how hard is it to let it go when it ends? And at the same time, how hard is it to be OK with something that caused us anger, or to just be sad?

In Vipassana meditation teaching there is a concept called *equanimity*, where you do not crave or cling to anything, but accept everything as it is, good or bad, equally. I personally think this is next to impossible, because we'll always favor the positive. But the point is to cling less to the positive, and accept that the bad times will end as well, so it's OK to have a few.

Practical Exercises

- ### <u>Feeling Your Emotions</u>

Most of us walk through life repressing our emotions. We push down those that are negative and pretend that things are "OK" when people ask us, putting on a fake smile. And when we feel good, sometimes we are so stuck in our heads that we can't be in the moment to enjoy things. We worry about the good thing ending, so we can't enjoy it NOW, or our brain invents reasons why this moment isn't good enough as it is.

You need to accept the reality as it is, not as you would like it to be.

This exercise will get you to begin to try and fully feel your emotions. This may be incredibly difficult if you have suppressed your needs or emotions for a very long time (for example, see the discussion of Nice Guy Syndrome in Chapter 32).

You have already been doing meditation, which is in effect learning to accept reality and be present, and not in your head. To go one step further, you will focus on feeling sensations in different parts of your body that usually carry emotions in them. You might feel the air in the room, temperature changes, muscular contractions. It does not matter, just focus on the area.

You must set aside 10 minutes a day to do this. I recommend doing this at night so you don't interfere with your regular practice, and so you can see how you feel after a day. Follow this plan:

- **Day 1** - Five minutes of Anapana meditation followed by five minutes of focusing on your mustache area.

- **Day 2** - Five minutes of Anapana meditation followed by five minutes of focusing on your throat area.

- **Day 3** - Five minutes of Anapana meditation followed by five minutes of focusing on your eyes.

- **Day 4** - Five minutes of Anapana meditation followed by five minutes of focusing on your jawline and lips.

- **Day 5** - Five minutes of Anapana meditation followed by five minutes of focusing on the area of your shoulders and upper back.

- **Day 6** - Five minutes of Anapana meditation followed by five minutes of focusing on your entire head area.

- **Day 7** - Ten minutes of focusing on any body part.

Each body part usually carries certain negative emotions:

The throat usually carries emotions of sadness, frustration, and anger. It is also a prime indicator of repressing words or emotions. When you focus on it, you may feel a "closing" or "choking."

The eyes usually withhold sadness. When you focus on them, you may feel like crying.

The jaw line and lips usually withhold tension and stress. When you focus on them, you may feel like clenching or your throat may tighten up.

The upper back and shoulders also withhold tension and stress. When you focus on them, you may feel your shoulders hunch up.

Your head can be associated with a range of negative emotions. When you focus on it, you may feel pain as you would a headache.

As most people withhold or repress negative emotions, I have outlined them here. Positive feelings are usually felt as pleasant tingling or "rain" on the body.

By learning to accept the sensations and not push them down, you learn to not repress your emotions and accept more of what is happening right now. You cannot change the present, only your reaction to it (accepting it and then moving forward).

In your journal you can write down what trouble spots you notice. What areas of your body feel particularly full of tension and do you NOT want to examine? What areas cause you to start feeling certain things? What are they?

As you continue to examine and let things go, you will become better at handling challenges and stress in your life because you realize most things are not a huge deal. The feeling will pass.

- **<u>Unsticking Negativity by Expanding Your Scope</u>**

Many times you might make the mistake of over-identifying so much with a powerful negative emotion in the present that you think that life is falling apart, things are terrible, and you have nothing. You let yourself be dragged down and your demeanor becomes terrible, to say the least.

It is important to not repress emotions, as they can never be thrown away. But that doesn't mean that life is that bad.

When something negative happens or you feel bad, answer the following questions. These are combined from exercises in previous sections, and you can refer to the pages listed for more detailed information. Following this chain will help you feel better. It can also be useful to examine things that seem so important now, but that really don't matter in the long run:

1. How big of a deal is this thing that is happening now? Will it really matter to me in two weeks, two months, or two years? (See "Problems in the Present Moment—Will This Matter in X Time", Chapter 24)

2. What is still good in life? What can I be grateful for? Has this really ruined my entire life? (See "Gratitude Exercise and Practice", Chapter 26)

3. Am I only looking at this in a negative way? Is there a positive I

can gain from this? A lesson or a benefit that will propel me forward?

4. Am I making some hurtful or unproven assumptions about the situation?

5. I have to remind myself that I've been happy before, and I'll be happy again. The bad times are going to pass because everything has to, so I'll be fine eventually (remember the **Law of Nature** at the beginning of this chapter?).

6. Make an action plan for any steps you need to take care of the situation. Ask: Can I change things if necessary?

7. How can I be kind to myself in this situation?

8. Go do something fun that takes you out of your head. Play sports, hang out with friends, do something just for you. I highly recommend trying to be with people if something is bothering you, because being alone will only allow your mind to take over you, while hanging out with positive people that love you and are not involved in your current issue can help give you some perspective.

9. If you need to, talk it out with these people.

Let's see two examples of this process in action with two common events you might go through:

Example #1

You go to a dinner with some friends and start chatting with a few people. You meet one person who you really hit it off with, and decide you would like to meet them some other time to see where things go. They get you, you laugh with them, and things are good! You exchange numbers and you both say you'll talk later.

You text the person and they don't respond. You know you

have the number right so you figure they're busy. But it's been two days and still nothing. You try again and still don't hear back.

What happened? This sucks. You feel a bit rejected, like your self-worth has been lowered, and that this person feigned interest.

Follow the chain:

1. Do I really think that I'll never meet anyone else? Do I think that I'll never date anyone else? How big is this problem compared to making sure that I am healthy, my bills are paid, and my job fulfills me?

2. Am I still reasonably healthy? I can probably still talk, travel, try amazing things in the world, and have use of many limbs. Some people live without an eye or a limb. I should be grateful that I have that. I can still afford food. Does not having one person like me make that much of an impact on my life? I should keep the scope in perspective.

3. Perhaps I misread the situation and we weren't getting along that well. Maybe this person was just interested in me for the night and not the long term. Maybe them not calling me is a way of saving myself time from chasing them because now I can focus on people who really want to see me. Maybe I didn't really do a good job differentiating myself or showing off my personality.

4. Maybe they got my messages and will call me back, but have gotten into an accident and are immobile at the hospital! Maybe they are genuinely busy and can't get back to me.

5. I have to remind myself that I've been happy before, and I'll be happy again. The bad times are going to pass because everything has to, so I'll be fine eventually.

6. If I wanted to, I could meet more people at different events throughout the week to have more options. I could use dating sites. Maybe I should do that instead of focusing on one person

who was not interested.

7. Some people don't even try to go on dates. I did well by at least talking to this person and trying to hang out with them. It's all good! I've still got my friends and family.

8. I should talk to my good friend to see if this is really worth stressing over. Maybe I should go to the gym too.

Notice here that, especially compared to not having a home or food, someone not calling you back seems like pretty small potatoes in the long run. By putting that into perspective, it helps get over smaller emotions much quicker.

Example #2

You are trying to find a new place to move to for a short period. You are worried about getting the best value for your buck while having good access to everything you need (e.g., a grocery store, the gym, and so on).

You move there and it's OK, but a bit farther than you thought from the gym. It's not the best to work at. You worry you won't be 100% happy there.

Following the chain again:

1. If I'm only going to be here for a short while, I can probably survive this. I mean, it's not all that bad. I still have lots of stuff around me, and I probably won't even remember these small inconveniences down the road. I'll probably just remember having a place to stay!

2. At least I can AFFORD a place to live. I mean, some people live on the street! I still have my own place to live, my own space to relax and reflect, and I have a comfy bed to sleep in too! I'm pretty sure I'll be fine.

3. Next time, I can try to do some more in-depth research on the locations of things around me in advance. I could also call the landlord if I really wanted to.

4. N/A

5. I have to remind myself that I've been happy before, and I'll be happy again. The bad times are going to pass because everything has to, so I'll be fine eventually (remember the **Law of Nature** at the beginning of this chapter?). I may have minor gripes with this place, but in the long haul I doubt it really matters!

6. If this place really bugs me, I can always cancel or pay a fine to get out. That would suck, but it's better than being incredibly unhappy. I guess if the gym is farther away I can see if I can swing my budget to allow me to have a transit pass to get there.

7. I did the best I could given the time and my knowledge and stress level. I can always learn for the next time I rent a place, and again, I'm only here for a bit! Not a huge deal!

8. I'm going to go for a walk and then go out with my friends later tonight. I know this will pass.

Both of these examples were taken from things I've gone through. Journaling specific events can be useful, ESPECIALLY at the start of unsticking. All of these steps are things that I do and remind myself to do as an event happens, but they are pretty habitual at this point. To begin building these habits, journaling to remind yourself of a proper order or some things you can do to expand your scope can be extremely helpful.

By learning that everything must pass, and hence there is no point in identifying with anything due to the **Law of Nature**, you can begin to move forward through challenges and troubling emotions much easier. Most things we think are big issues are really impactful in the moment, but over the long run are really quite small issues.

Worry about handling the bigger things and don't sweat the small stuff. Most things fall into the category of "small stuff."

Chapter 34.
Comparing Yourself to Others

"He has an awesome girlfriend, I've got no one."
"She's so much prettier than me."
"Why can't I be less afraid, like my friend?"

One of the MOST unfair things you can do is compare yourself to someone else.

Why You Might Do It and Where It Comes From

Unfortunately, in society today we are raised to battle, compete with, and compare ourselves to those around us. It starts in school with standardized testing and competitive scoring, and it is also instinctual in our biology. For example, with men in tribes, the strongest men got all the women. With that being the case, each man in the tribe would constantly try to be better than other men to succeed in spreading his seed.

Of course, we are all technically still in competition, and we do get compared to others by potential mates, job contractors, and so on. It's inevitable, and something that goes on in the background of life.

But the thing is, when you let that be at the forefront of how you set up your life and function, you will ALWAYS be in an uphill battle. There will ALWAYS be someone better than you at something. If you have focused your life on becoming a Nobel Prize-winning scientist, an Olympian will be better than you at sports. If you spend most of your time practicing ballet, a violinist will obviously be better at playing violin. Even at something you spend hours on and are amazing at, there will always be someone better than you, and you can always learn more. You can always be better.

What's the Positive Alternative to Boost Your Mental Energy?

In self-improvement there's a method of living that I call "keeping your reference frame internal, except for slight glimpses." This means that you look to what others have achieved to show that something is possible, but you refrain from getting jealous or annoyed at them for achieving it. Rather, you use them as inspiration and motivation to show you that if you put in the time and work, you can achieve something too.

But there are several things to keep in mind:

- As humans, we have the ability to set our OWN standards of success. It makes sense for a violinist to say that if she practices four hours a day and gets into the Philharmonic orchestra, she is successful. But someone training for the Olympics has other goals in mind, such as nutrition and track time. In this sense, the paradigm society places on us of there being ONE way to measure success (i.e., via a test score) is flawed, broken, and useless.

Begin to ask yourself, "What do I think would be my definition of success? What do I want to achieve in my life?" Not only will this be more fulfilling, but it will also help you locate the things that are more important and fun for you.

- Every person is born with the same set of beliefs and is an innocent child, sparing extreme circumstances. It is only through traumatic events and experiences that we inherit our "weaknesses" that make us wish we were "less scared than someone else," "smarter," and so on.

It is completely unfair to compare yourself to someone else. You have both been through entirely different lives and, as such, you're in different places. EVERYONE has anxieties that cripple them, and problems. It's just that different people have ones that affect them more than others.

If you spent most of your life indoors in front of a computer, and being bullied, why would you think it fair to compare yourself to someone who has been extremely popular, pushed to meet other people, and extroverted in character their entire life?

- While you can achieve anything you put your mind to, different people are gifted with different abilities that make it easier for them to achieve certain goals. Arnold Schwarzenegger became a muscle-bound bodybuilder at a young age. If I really wanted to, I could achieve that, but my genes keep me small despite eating a lot and working out. If I really focused, ate all the time, and set this as my priority, I could achieve it. But it would take EXTREME amounts of effort because I am less genetically inclined to become big.

On the other hand, I inherited my dad's intelligence and work ethic for logic-based work, and my mom's aptitude for music and understanding rhythm. Sure, a great deal of this was learned too, but I have a natural inclination to learning intellectual topics other people find boring, and music runs in my blood. Arnie is also a smart guy, but he didn't pursue an engineering degree because he had other goals in mind. He could have done it, but it might have taken him a lot more effort to get the exact same results I did.

Practical Exercises

Many times, comparison to others can be born from a low sense of self-esteem and self-worth. Building those up can drastically decrease comparison. We also often miss all that we have, thinking there is so much we don't have, or NEED to survive. So thinking about what you already own and being grateful for it can really help as well.

Refer to:

- The section **self-criticism and negative self-talk** (Chapter 29) and the exercises there.

- The *Gratitude Exercise and Practice* in the **jealousy and envy** section (Chapter 26)

As you begin to discover how much you already have, and as you become less self-critical, you will compare yourself to others less and less.

Comparison Drive

As noted, comparison can be a POSITIVE force to say, "*If they did that, I can too!*" Turn that comparison into a positive force and create an action plan to do something about it. See *Why Am I Jealous and What Am I Going to Do About It?* in Chapter 26.

It doesn't mean you will never compare. It means you are beaten down less and less by it because you know you already have so much, but can continually improve your life to have more amazing things. The "need to have more" drive never goes away, as humans are wired to be perpetually unhappy—it keeps us alive and always creating more. Those that never strive to be better will be weeded out of the gene pool, since they will never improve, create, or move forward.

Know that no external item, such as a car, a book deal, or a girlfriend, will ever bring you happiness. Happiness lies within the pursuit of the items that mean something to you, or the pursuit of a good life. It's about the journey, not the end goal.

As Mark Manson said:

"If life is a hamster wheel, then the goal isn't to actually get anywhere, it's to find a way to enjoy running.[1]"

165

---

[1] Manson, Mark. *9 Subtle Lies We All Tell Ourselves.* markmanson.net. Retrieved from http://markmanson.net/9-subtle-lies-we-all-tell-ourselves on January 7th, 2015.

Chapter 35.
Rushing

"I have to take the kids here. Then I gotta go to the gym. Then I gotta do the work. Oh man, I can cut corners here.
AHHHHHHHHHHHHH."

Society today moves at a breakneck speed.

Why is it that we have so much technology to make our lives easier, to move us to places faster, to keep us in touch with loved ones across miles and miles, yet anxiety and depression are at an all-time high? Approximately 185 million people suffer from depression, and 334 million suffer from anxiety.[1]

There is no time for going outside, exercising, or taking lunch. There are mounting deadlines and 80-hour workweeks.

Once in a while this might be acceptable, but what happens when this is a habit? If this is life?

It's routine for you to be hard on yourself for sleeping in a bit. It's routine for you to cut breaks. It's routine for you to burn yourself out so much that you can't see your friends after work, and all you want to do is veg out in front of the TV.

You only have one life, and you should milk AS MUCH out of it as possible. But there must be a limit to how fast you move. Otherwise, if you haven't smelled the roses or have spent so much time rushing, you'll wake up one day and ask, "Where did it all go?"

Why You Might Do It and Where It Comes From

I am quite guilty of rushing at times, and in my opinion this can come from several sources:

- **Over-scheduling and over-extending yourself**. Putting too much into one day.

- **Perfectionism**. Assigning goals and tasks and NEEDING those to be done. Expecting a strict schedule to always be kept. One needs to be perfect and get things done, otherwise...

- **Self-criticism**. You are bad if you don't do enough. Yet even if you accomplish what you set out to do, you could have done more. Begin vicious circle of beating yourself up.

You believe that if you don't get your work done, then you are bad. But this is only the case if you believe you ARE your work. Even for someone who owns their own company, they are NOT the company—they are the person behind it.

If, in childhood, you believed that you were bad, you may have become synergized with external factors (which in adulthood can translate into your work, your car, etc.) to prove your worth. Even if you are bad, your car is great, so it's not a big deal if you screw up because the car will always be nice. In that sense, you rush to get tasks done.

David Deida notes in *Way of the Superior Man* how men specifically get stuck in "to-do" mode, and how they believe that if they just work enough or get enough done, something will change. They believe they can do enough in one day. The dirty truth is that nobody can do enough in one day—there is always more that can be done.

Many times, people will use the "being busy" excuse as a method for covering up fears or holes in their life. It can also be a way to rush through not feeling things. Workaholics apply here! For example, I used schoolwork as a means to cover up my social anxiety and loneliness throughout undergrad: Amazing grades, excellent job out of school, placement into one of the top graduate schools in the world, but zero dates, a lot of missed times with friends, and explorative years gone. I made up for it later though, so don't worry about me!

What's the Positive Alternative to Boost Your Mental Energy?

The answer is simple, yet complicated: Stop rushing.

So many amazing things happen, yet you are often so caught up in the future that you miss what is right in front of you. As I am writing this book I feel a tendency to worry that I won't get some other work done, yet this writing is extremely important to me and takes time. And also, I'm writing a freakin' book! I get to write what I think will help people be happier, and I get to learn tons of new things while doing it. So, how could I rush it?

In productivity and goal setting, everyone says to set deadlines, otherwise things will just drag on. Parkinson's Law says you will take as much time on a given task as you have assigned for it. There are very good tips about turning your cell phone off and closing your e-mail so you don't get distracted and don't procrastinate.

I believe these things all have their place and it takes time, testing, and determining what works for you to see how you can use these to your advantage.

But the main thing it comes down to is **acceptance**. Accept that:

1. You are human, and may not get as much done as you want to in a day.

2. There is only so much time in one day, so you must prioritize what is important to you.

3. A bit of missed time here and there will not matter in two

months, and especially not in two years.

4. Work expands to fill your time, and there's always tomorrow to do it.

Practical Exercises

- <u>**This Is Important Now**</u>

When you find yourself rushing and worrying about getting to the next thing, realize that what you are doing is important right now. If it's not important, then stop doing it or get someone else to do it. Don't waste your time on things that make you go *"Eh, this is OK."* If you can't get someone else to do it right now, figure out a way so that in the future you won't have to do it, and put your full attention to it right now to get it done well.

- <u>**Three Things Today**</u>

Usually people have issues determining what they need to do, so they waste time on e-mail or other busy work and feel terrible because they've accomplished nothing at the end of the day. Before the beginning of the workday, or the night before, write down the three priorities of the day and focus on getting those things done. Do not add more than three things. Try and get those things done, and be happy when you do.

- <u>**Scheduling Stops**</u>

Morning meditation is a stop. Time with loved ones is a stop. Doing a passion is a stop. Energy is cyclic, and if you keep rushing from thing to thing, from work to more work, you will burn out extremely fast. To replenish your energy, spend your off time with people and things that you love. Cut out all the crap that, again, makes you go "Eh"—and be ruthless about it. Unless it makes you go "OH MY GOD," it's not necessary and can be gotten rid of.

For extreme type-A personalities (such as me!), you need to

SCHEDULE stops. I have a calendar that I schedule my time in, and if I don't have my stops (exercise, drums, dates, hanging out with friends), the time will be filled with useless things.

The scheduled stops also help with feeling your emotions. As you learned, they can never be repressed. They will either come out in backhanded or side ways, or you can directly feel and express them.

Try writing down the times you set aside for your stops and holding yourself accountable to see if you actually did them. If you did, how did you feel after? If you didn't, why couldn't you? What reasons did you have to not stop? What did you think might happen?

And most importantly, did it?

- **<u>One Day Off</u>**

This is not negotiable.

Life moves so fast that we usually have no time to be introspective, which can be a way of hiding troubling emotions. Rushing and working all the time also completely depletes your energy and causes burnout. Just like emotions, you can't push aside rest time. It will come out one way or another. But if that's the case, you might as well SCHEDULE it.

Your day off should be completely devoid of any responsibility. It is a reward for working your butt off during the week. It is a time to do things you love, spend time with awesome people, try new things, and so on.

If you have one day off where you aren't working towards something, and then work the other six days (either on things that make you money, or doing errands), that still means 86% of your time is devoted to working. I think that's still extremely fair, especially if it will allow you to accomplish more, and in a much quicker span of time!

- **<u>What Is Important to Me</u>**

This is an exercise that only needs to be done once in a while. It is a modified version of something Mark Manson suggested in his old document called the *Life Purpose Guide*[2].

Take out a sheet of paper and draw a table with three columns: activity, time, and happiness value.

Write down ALL the things you do during the week. Don't include things like brushing your teeth, but things like "watching YouTube," "being with girlfriend," "cooking," and so on.

Then write down the approximate time it takes...maybe per day, or per week. Estimate the hours.

Now on a value of 0-10, rank how happy the activity makes you. For example, here are some of mine:

Activity	Time	Happiness Value
Watching YouTube	8+ hours/week	2
Drumming	2 hours/week	9
Being with friends	8 hours/week	9
Working - blogging, writing books, marketing, etc.	35 hours/week	8
Errands	3 hours/week	3
Cooking and grocery shopping	5 hours/week	2
Going to the gym	6 hours/week	8
Actively reading a specific book	1 hour/week	8

After doing this, look at the list. What you are looking for are huge outliers. So for me, drumming is only two hours a week but gives me a happiness value of nine, so I should find ways to increase this. The same goes for reading a book I am working on.

However, YouTube only gives me a happiness value of two, and I spend a lot of time on it. Thus, I should decrease that (believe me, I've tried, and keep on having to stop myself). The same goes for cooking and grocery shopping.

In this way, you can find mismatches of time and happiness and work to limit what does not give you that much happiness. Or, you can find a way to put the low happiness thing with something that gives you a lot of happiness if you know you're going to do it either way. For example, if video games are a habit of yours but don't give you much happiness, yet you know you're always going to be drawn to them, you can make sure you play video games with friends (assuming hanging out with your friends makes you happy).

You can also strategize ways to get your needs met. I sometimes have problems seeing my friends as much as I want to, so if I pay a few bucks to head to an office where they are, it's worth it (in my opinion).

You might have issues letting go of an activity that doesn't give you a lot of happiness, but that you are drawn to. If this is the case, I suggest using a technique from the book by Chip and Dan Heath, *Decisive*, and asking, *"What could I do instead with this time that I am spending here?"* Perhaps that might help you get out of the habit of spending time where you don't want to. If watching TV doesn't make you happy and you feel your life draining away, yet you spend hours on it, imagine that you could be reading books, going on dates, learning how to cook, and so on instead. That might snap you into your senses.

Tim Ferriss, one of my most prominent influences, said to work hard, but always recommended taking a night every week to have dinner with friends.

Why?

Life moves so fast, and we're always pushed to do more. And then, as soon as we know it, time is gone and we can't do anything. So then we wish we had enjoyed our time while we were here.

Nobody ever regretted taking a day off work when they were on their deathbed.

Tim was lambasted by some people for his book *The Four-Hour Work Week*, and falsely advertising that you could start a business working just four hours a week. Actually, Tim said that it would take lots of work. The point of the book was to outsource and kill crap that you didn't want to do in life so you had more time for what and who WAS important. And, to maximize your per hour work output. It was also to call into the spotlight the way most Western jobs are aligned: Work 50 weeks a year, limited sick time, limited vacation time, etc. It doesn't seem fair at all.

A prime conclusion in this section should be that you can only do so much work a day, you only have so much time, you can only move so fast, and that's OK. You just have to make the most of it. Maximize your happiness by doing the things that make you feel alive, and spend time with the people who fill you with joy.

Cut the rest of the crap out.

---

[1] Figures calculated using population data from World Bank (http://data.worldbank.org/) and anxiety statistics from The Mental Health Foundation (http://www.mentalhealth.org.uk/help- information/mental-health-statistics/anxiety-statistics/), both retrieved November 7th, 2014.

[2] You can download this guide here (http://markmanson.net/content/PDFs/Life_Purpose_Guide.pdf).

Conclusion

You've learned a lot over the course of this book:

You've gone over how you need to have a logical part of you calming the emotional part down, and how your thoughts create your mood and reality. You've learned how to meditate as well. You then learned about 19 mental wastes, why they are hurting you, and how to change them into fuel to make you stronger and better.

I have tried to provide you with as many tools as I can to eliminate these wastes, but self-improvement is extremely personal—what works for one, does not work for someone else. You will need to experiment to find out what works for you, and it will take time. But, I am confident that with some drive, patience, and a positive attitude towards learning, you will get where you need to. You won't be perfect, you might fall down, but as long as you get back up—you're winning. Becoming a happy, healthy, human being is the by-product of taking care of your life, doing what you want, and also dealing with your emotions in a mature and strategic manner.

There are three other points I want to leave you with:

First, an important thing to keep in mind as you work is to always, always, always **accept things as they are**. Sure, you might not deal with jealousy that well, but at least you have some tools to deal with it now. You can go get what you want. You also have tools to deal with the fear that comes from going after what you want. You might not want to accept that things can be difficult to achieve, that life should be different, that you shouldn't be as anxious, that you need help sometimes...

But this is all OK.

You're getting stronger, trying to improve, and you will change. Look back at your journal over the weeks, months, and years and see how you've changed. How have you grown? Trust me, the results will be mind boggling.

Second, that life will throw you curve balls you don't expect. Some will be just annoying, others may be quite depressing and difficult to deal with. **You can't control what happens, you can only control your reactions to the events.** Trying to control life just leads to stress. So control your boundaries on work hours to keep yourself in a peaceful state, limit your contact with negative things and people, always look on the bright side of things (because there usually is a bright side), and ensure you take time to re-charge with friends, family, doing the things you love, or laughing your ass off to a good comedy.

Finally:

Life is short. I'm going to assume that I'm only here once and I want to try and be as happy as I can. I might not be perfect, but I'm learning how to make myself happier, and I always try to consider the glass half full. Yes this is a bit trite, but it's important. In the world of emotions and perception, you still get to decide if what you feel and do is good, so always choose the positive interpretation and go make your dreams a reality.

Good luck and be happy.

Extras

Chapter 36.
Extra #1 - Test If You're Wasting Mental Energy Now

You might be wondering how to know if you are wasting mental energy right now.

What's the quickest way you can check without THINKING about if you are or not?

Well, ask yourself one simple question:

"What am I thinking about?"

What's the answer?

Got it?

If the answer is anything but **nothing**, there's a 99.9% chance you are wasting mental energy.

Remember: The mind does not exist in the present, only in the past (with regret) or in the future (with anxiety).

Our goal was to find out if you are wasting mental energy, how to get out of it, but then to come back to the present. You can't live in your mind.

So if you are thinking, chances are that there's some waste going on.

Of course, we need to think to create complex work. Our minds can do amazing things, but random thoughts are usually counter-productive.

As you progress along the path of spirituality, meditation, and self-improvement, you'll be able to figure out faster if you are wasting energy or not. Everyone gets stuck in their thoughts sometimes, and that's OK. But usually, thinking and churning won't get you anywhere.

Chapter 37.
Extra #2 - How to Raise Your Mental Energy in Eight Easy Steps

You learned ways that you might be causing yourself stress by over thinking and being too involved with your thoughts. By implementing the exercises in working towards the positive alternatives to wastes, you can start flying.

But are there some other methods to give you a little boost in life?

Here are some of my suggestions:

- **Stop associating with negative people**

Complainers, those who are happy just scraping by, people who (negatively) criticize you, people who don't lift you up... What the hell is the point in being brought down by them? Focus on the few people who make you feel amazing, and don't let anyone else in.

If you can't get rid of someone completely (such as a family member), then limit your contact with them. This sounds selfish, but you have to look out for yourself and your well-being. You can't be afraid of hurting someone's feelings.

- **Get away from the news**

What makes most people stick to the screen? Information about car crashes, fights, and strife. That's what the news typically plays. Tragedy sells.

Get away from there.

Start relying on other people to tell you if something important is going on, or use things like the uplifting news Sub-Reddit [1] to get your news fix.

- **Cut out bad food**

Garbage (McDonald's, deep fried onion rings, processed sugar) in, garbage (sugar crashes, upset stomach, bad mood) out. Start eating whole foods. Take three hours on one day and cook your food for the week, storing it in your fridge or freezer for use. That way, you can quickly put meals together, and don't have to worry about eating poorly.

Side benefit: This is far cheaper than eating out all of the time.

- **Watch motivational speeches**

There are people who are paid to motivate and inspire you. I recently started listening to these speeches at the gym, and oh boy do I feel AMAZING afterwards. I sometimes listen to one in the morning as well. Some popular speakers to check out:

1. Les Brown

2. Anthony Robbins

3. Arnold Schwarzenegger

4. Eric Thomas (ET)

You can just search "inspirational speeches" and add their names at the end. Or, pick a subject you want to be inspired or hear them talk about, and Google or YouTube their name with that at the end of the search query.

- **Clean up your place**

Messy environment = messy mind. Keep your place clean and organized, and get some damn sunlight in there. Your mind will become clearer.

- **Get outside**

Speaking of sunlight, we spend too much time in cubicles and offices bombarded by artificial light. Get outside and stretch your legs, breathe in the air, and walk around some green space. As a byproduct, you will feel more relaxed and present.

- **Positive slogans/backgrounds/notes and affirmations**

Another idea is to stick positive affirmations around your workplace, house, and as backgrounds for your computer. You can also use images of places you'd love to visit, or things that inspire you. These should be personal and related to things you're working on incorporating into your life. Some of mine include:

"This too shall change—it's not a big deal."

Screenshots of my degrees.

"Don't let idiots ruin your day."

Pictures of Asian cities.

"Follow your passion and success will follow you."

"Just do it."

- **Listen to uplifting and/or relaxing music**

Violent and harsh music will affect your brainwaves. I used to listen to lots of metal, with screaming, chugging guitars, and some questionable lyrics. I refuse to give it up for drumming (I haven't found anything that matches the technicality or energy), but during my workday or while relaxing, I'm usually listening to ambient electronica, EDM, or softer rap. It makes me happier, more relaxed, and more productive.

Of course, music preferences are different for everybody. Some people might prefer classical or country. The point is to find music with a positive sound and message.

By implementing even a selection of these items into your life you can start to increase your mental energy passively.

---

[1] See: http://www.reddit.com/r/UpliftingNews/.

Chapter 38.
Extra #3 - A Primer on Goal Setting

Setting goals is an essential skill and part of life. I like to say, "If you don't know what you're working towards, where the hell are you going?" That doesn't mean you don't enjoy life right now, but it does mean you need to have a clear idea in your mind of where you want to get.

I highly recommend looking at Mark Manson's *Life Purpose Report*[1] for some help in figuring out where you want your life to go. I go through it every year and have found it extremely useful in propelling me forward.

Setting goals might not be sexy, but by following a few tips you can make things far clearer and easier for yourself, SKYROCKETING your chances of success. Here are some helpful hints when you do decide to sit down:

- **Don't set more than three to four goals at once**. You might get excited to make drastic changes in your life, set a bunch of goals, and try to do them all at once. There's no way you can keep up with all of these, and then you fail. A negative self-critical cycle begins. So...

- **Focus on one or two goals at a time**. Some goals might overlap, but don't spread yourself too thin. If your goal is to develop a habit, build a website, or something of that nature, focus, do it, and pat yourself on the back when you've done it. This requires a GREAT deal of patience and persistence.

- **Make goals very clear and defined**. For instance, "make money online" is not clear. "Make $1,000 from my drop-shipping business by April 1st" is. You have:

    - A numerical amount

- A deadline

- A specific method by which you want to accomplish it

This does not mean that the goal can't change (maybe you decide not to do drop shipping, but writing books instead), but this clarity allows you to focus and drive forward.

- **Use rewards**. Always be kind and reward yourself. Once you hit a goal or benchmark, give yourself something (and that something is up to you!). A massage, a half a day off work, a new toy, etc. Make the reward proportional to the goal. Don't buy yourself coffee if you finish a book that took you a year to write, and don't buy yourself a car for writing 30 minutes today. But either way, reward yourself every step of the way. This teaches your brain that work leads to pleasure, and then you become excited to get work done.

- **Always make sure your goal is for you and NOT to impress others.** If a goal is for external reasons (validation, like people saying you are amazing for starting a business), it will probably fail. If it's for something that you really want, something you love, or something you see as an investment for yourself and the future, you are more likely to push through obstacles and have a blast while doing it.

- **Set lower/easier goals**. If you set massive ones, you might not realize the amount of time and "grinding" that needs to be input, and you'll lose motivation along the way. If you set smaller goals or benchmarks, you get a bit of motivation along the way as you are working. If you believe something is easier, you will be able to make yourself work towards it with less effort. If it seems hard, your brain will trick you into thinking it's impossible, and you will never start. For example: Instead of saying, *"I want to publish a book"* (yes, keep that as the end goal!), use benchmarks:

  - Write 30 minutes a day.

- Finish a draft by X date.

- Hire an editor.

- Proofread it myself.

- Find someone to do a cover.

- Etc.

In this sense, the HUGE goal of publishing a book is broken down into smaller, easier steps.

Another way to look at goals is to think of the habits you can implement to make the goals a reality. For example, setting a habit of writing 30 minutes a day to get the book draft done. Ensuring you go to the gym three times a week to add on that 10 pounds of muscle. The topics of habits and habit setting is a separate discussion and beyond the scope of this book, but there are many excellent resources to learn about habit setting, including Mark Manson's free e-book[2].

---

[1] You can download the guide here (http://markmanson.net/content/PDFs/ Life_Purpose_Guide.pdf).

[2] You can download this by click here (http://markmanson.net/habits).

About Noam Lightstone

Noam Lightstone was born in Ottawa, Ontario, Canada, and graduated with a Master's degree from the University Of Toronto in 2014.

After being involved in self-improvement for several years and finding tools that greatly improved his quality of life and overall happiness, he decided to share his knowledge with others and turn his personal blog, Light Way Of Thinking, into his full-time career. The resource focuses on helping individuals overcome anxiety and depression to live full and amazing lives. His work focuses on 3 principles:

1. Cultivating emotional connections with others

So you will never feel lonely or misunderstood.

2. Cultivating an emotional connection with yourself, and working towards what your ideal life and vision is

So you know you are living the best life possible, in congruence with your dreams and aspirations.

3. Learning to work with your mind/thoughts and emotions

So you can properly express yourself, do not get caught up over thinking, and do not become stifled.

Noam currently lives a mobile lifestyle, traveling and residing across the world. He currently lives in Ho Chi Minh City, Vietnam, as of February 2015. You can find more about Noam and read his work at his blog, Light Way Of Thinking (http://www.lightwayofthinking.com).

Made in the USA
San Bernardino, CA
03 March 2017